The Sporting Royal Family

THE SPORTING ROYAL FAMILY

with photographs by
SERGE LEMOINE
and text by
GRANIA FORBES

QUEEN ANNE PRESS
MACDONALD & CO (PUBLISHERS) LTD
LONDON & SYDNEY

Produced by Robert Dudley and John Stidolph
Designed by John Robinson
© Antler Books 1982
First published in 1982 by Queen Anne Press
a division of Macdonald & Co (Publishers) Ltd
Holywell House, Worship Street, London EC2A 2EN

ISBN 0356 08603 8

All rights reserved. No part of this publication may be reproduced, stored in a retrieval system or transmitted in any form or by any means electronic, mechanical, photocopying or otherwise without the prior permission of the copyright owner.

Typesetting by Inforum Ltd, Portsmouth, England
Colour separations by Nickeloid Litho, London
Printed in Italy by New Interlitho SPA, Milan

Prince Andrew after successfully completing his first solo glider flight

Frontispiece: Lt Philip Mountbatten in the nets

CONTENTS

Acknowledgements	6
The Outdoor Life	9
A Love of the Turf	23
Polo	43
Carriage Driving	63
Eventing and Showjumping	79
Making a Splash	91
Winter Sports	103
Field Sports	113

The Prince, like all his family, is versatile. Here he is playing hockey in Oxford

Prince Charles shooting pool in the Pear Tree Coffee Bar, Derby

ACKNOWLEDGEMENTS

The author, photographer and producers of this book would like to thank the following for their help and advice during its compilation: Michael Shea, Anne Wall and the staff of the Press Office at Buckingham Palace; Lt Col Sir Martin Gilliat and Major John Griffin; the staff of the Press Association, particularly Mr & Mrs Jack Richards, Paddy Hicks and Ronald Bell; Beth Barrington-Haynes, Major Ronald Ferguson, Raymond Brooks-Ward, and the staffs of the Sporting Life, the British Horse Society and the British Carriage Driving Society.

The Queen Mother playing snooker in the Press Club

Serge Lemoine has been a 'royal' photographer since 1964 when he left *Paris Match*, where he had been the London *chef de bureau*, to concentrate full time on photography. Since then he has established a reputation as one of the foremost visual reporters of the activities of the Royal Family in the world, and editors of leading magazines in Europe and the USA vie with each other for his pictures.

Action pictures are a particular speciality of Serge Lemoine and this collection gives a good indication of his talent. In the course of his career he has covered no less than fifty-five Royal Tours including, most recently, the Queen's visit to Australia and New Zealand.

Although he was born in France, he has now set up home permanently in England where he has lived for the last twenty years.

Grania Forbes joined the Press Association in 1974 and has been Court Correspondent, accredited to Buckingham Palace since 1978. She is therefore in an ideal position to observe the Royal Family at close quarters and to follow the different sports and games pursued by each of them.

Grania Forbes herself is a keen sportswoman who enjoys sailing and skiing and until recently exercised polo ponies in Richmond Park. She writes knowledgeably about all aspects of royal life, but the subject of this book is one that is close to her heart.

She is married and has one child – a son.

THE OUTDOOR LIFE

Princess Anne, who has won many trophies, was particularly happy to receive a prize from her mother at the Windsor Horse Show

A LOVE of exercise and the outdoor life has been part of the tradition of the royal family at least since the time of Queen Victoria. The royal archive contains hundreds of sketches made by the Queen on the frequent walks she took through the Scottish heather with her notebook and water colours. Though she herself was not exactly a sportswoman in the sense that her children and grandchildren were, she encouraged all her family in the usual country pursuits of hunting and shooting and towards the end of her life she took to riding around her estates in a dog cart. Whether the present Duke of Edinburgh's enthusiasm for carriage driving can be traced back to this is open to question. One of the earliest cine films made vividly records the royal progress, cinematography being another of Queen Victoria's passions.

Opposite: The Prince of Wales inspects the course before competing in a cross country riding event

Queen Victoria in her pony carriage at Balmoral. She is attended by George Gordon, a lady-in-waiting, and an Indian orderly Abdul Khayrim

Edward VII at Epsom for the Derby in 1909. On the right is the Prince of Wales (later George V)

George V riding at Windsor accompanied by his four sons, Albert Duke of York (later George VI), Henry Duke of Gloucester, George Duke of Kent and Edward Prince of Wales (later Edward VIII, subsequently Duke of Windsor)

Edward VII on the other hand was a sportsman in the fullest sense of the word. It was he, on his return from a grand tour of India, who began to build up a stable that was the foundation of the royal family's interest in racing.

It was Edward who, as a keen sailor, had the cutter Britannia specially built for him in the 1890's. The boat was raced with a considerable degree of success and in his later years the King regularly presided at the Cowes Regatta. On his retirement he was accorded the honorary position of Admiral of the Royal Yacht Squadron.

Edward enjoyed most of the contemporary sports of his time, tennis, golf, hunting and motor car driving. But his great love was shooting. With the help of the Earl of Leicester, Sandringham was built up into one of the most prolific pheasant and partridge shoots in the country. Grouse shooting was equally to his taste. It was said that any social climber had only to purchase a grouse moor where a bag of a thousand or more could be recorded to be sure of securing the King's acceptance to an invitation.

The Prince of Wales and his brother Prince Albert playing golf in 1920

The Duke of York with his new wife (now Queen Elizabeth the Queen Mother), playing golf on their honeymoon in 1923

Edward Prince of Wales, preparing to compete in the Army Point-to-Point in 1924, with his brothers Prince Albert and Prince Henry who was acting as a steward

Below left: The Duke of York playing in the Wimbledon Championships in 1926

Below: The Duke of York in 1933, three years before becoming King

Prince Charles sweeps a ball to leg when playing in a charity cricket match for Lord Brabourne against a team of grand-prix drivers

Prince William of Gloucester, just before taking off for the race in which he died when his plane crashed on 28 August 1972

Prince Andrew makes contact with an opponent while playing rugby for Lakefield College in Canada

Royal devotion to both shooting and riding continued with George V but Edward VIII was the first monarch actually to compete in a horse race. He started in point-to-point racing and his racing career reached its climax on April Fool's Day in 1920 when, on Pet Dog, he won the Welsh Guards' Challenge Cup at Hawthorne Hill racing under National Hunt rules.

It was said that he never acquired a strong seat on a horse and this, coupled with a determination to jump every obstacle that came his way, gave him the reputation of one who was easily separated from his mount. By the late 1920's pressure from his family, politicians and the press forced him to give up riding.

Edward VIII was a keen huntsman and started another family tradition by playing polo. He also played golf, skied and swam and reached the final of the Squash Rackets Handicap at the Bath Club.

George VI shared his brother's enthusiasm for golf, achieving a handicap of ten. He played both golf and cricket left-handed and proof of his prowess as a cricketer is still on display at the Royal Naval College Dartmouth where can be seen the ball with which, in successive deliveries, he dismissed King Edward VII, King George V and the Duke of Windsor. He was a fine tennis player also and scored a notable royal first when, as Duke of York, he appeared in the first round of the men's doubles at Wimbledon in June 1926.

His two great passions however were shooting and the turf. He

Gary Sobers, the great West Indian cricketer receives his knighthood from the Queen

Opposite: Lucinda Prior-Palmer, four times winner at Badminton, receives the Whitbread Trophy from the Queen as Prince Andrew and Prince Philip look on

was a successful owner. In 1942 his horses won four of the five classics, the Two Thousand Guineas, the One Thousand Guineas, the Oaks and the St. Leger. In 1946 he won the One Thousand Guineas again with Hyperium and Above Board, another of his horses, won the Cesarewitch.

The King was a fine shot with a beautiful action and a deadly aim. He loved shooting at Balmoral and at Sandringham, particularly duck, and was out with his gun the day before he died.

The present royal family share the sporting enthusiasms of their predecessors and have added some of their own. The Queen and her mother have a deep love of horses, and both have become experts on blood lines. The Queen has bred many winners.

The Queen and the Queen Mother like walking. The Queen Mother has been known to go out in the teeth of a gale and on a recent visit to Australia on one of her days off, the Queen went on a seven mile trek through east Tasmania. Prince Charles also enjoys walking as was shown by his recent ten day walk through the Himalayas.

Prince Charles, who was captain of the soccer team while at his preparatory school Cheam, is an all-round sportsman, and plays most games well. During the long summer holidays in Scotland at Balmoral Castle the Prince goes out shooting and stalking, – activities which recently caused an uproar in the anti-bloodsports lobby when the Princess of Wales went with him.

Members of the royal family enjoying an early morning ride on Ascot race course. Left to right are the Duke of Beaufort, the Queen, the Hon Angus Ogilvy, the Countess of Lichfield and Prince Charles

Like other families with country estates, all the royal family go hunting and shooting but with as little publicity as possible to avoid offending some of their more sensitive subjects.

Prince Andrew and Prince Edward enjoy shooting and both have been seen out with a gun at Sandringham. Prince Andrew competed in a clay pigeon shooting match with Captain Mark Phillips in the Royals v Lords match in 1980.

Prince Andrew, who scored two goals the first time he played ice hockey in Canada, is said to be a useful fullback at rugby as well as playing tennis and soccer well. He and his brother Prince Edward, also like cricket and have been practising in the nets at Lords.

Prince Andrew was coached at Wimbledon by Dan Maskell and of course all the Kent family take a great interest in tennis. The Duke of Kent is president of the Lawn Tennis Association and usually presents the cups after the final.

Prince Michael of Kent used to prefer more dangerous sports. He captained Britain's Olympic bobsleigh team and is now president of the British Bobsleigh Association. In 1970 he entered the

Opposite: The Duchess of Kent has a deep knowledge and love of tennis. Here she presents the Ladies' Singles Trophy to Evonne Cawley at Wimbledon

London to Mexico World Cup Rally but his part ended when his Maxi car left the road in Brazil. He later competed in the Daily Express Ford Championship and the Devil's Own Rally before rallying against the world champion driver James Hunt in the Avon Tour of Britain.

The Gloucester family can also produce a turn of speed although of a rather different kind. The Duke and Duchess are expert skiers and frequently accompany the Prince of Wales to the slopes.

Princess Alexandra and her family prefer water sports. They rarely miss the royal regatta at Cowes and the Princess and her children are frequently seen out sailing.

Prince Michael of Kent with Gavin Thompson and Nigel Clarkson preparing for the World Cup Rally in 1970

Opposite: Prince Charles in the Australian outback

Monaveen, the Queen's first racehorse, A Grantham up, takes the last fence in the Queen Elizabeth Chase at Hurst Park in 1949

A LOVE OF THE TURF

THE QUEEN's great-grandfather, King Edward VII, was once described as the brother of all racegoers. His three Derby wins and his victory in the Grand National were triumphs in which the whole country shared. It was said that his passion for racing was one of the things that made him so popular. Certainly it was a financial success. In 1900 as Prince of Wales, he headed the list of owners with winnings of £29,586 – the equivalent of more than £100,000 today.

The Queen has carried on this royal success story with over 300 winners to date and in 1954 became the first British monarch since Charles II to head the list of winning owners. As Princess Elizabeth, she started in partnership with the Queen Mother. The royal ladies bought an Irish bred Steeplechaser called Monaveen for £1,000 on the recommendation of trainer Peter Cazalet and on 29 September 1949 the registration was published in the *Racing Calendar*.

Opposite: A thrilling moment in the Royal Box during the Derby

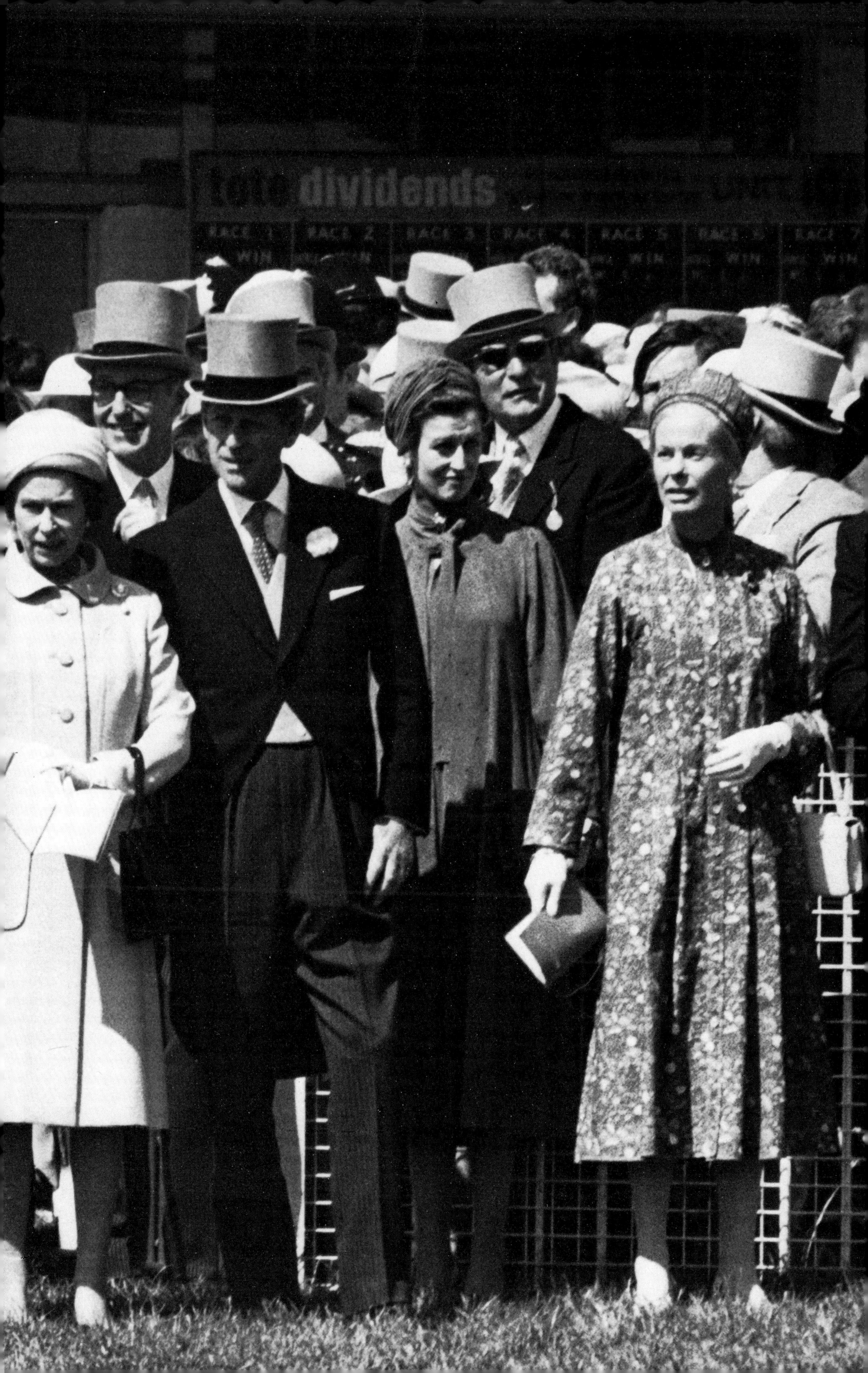
tote dividends

The Queen's Aureole, E Smith up, wearing the royal colours

The famous moment when Devon Loch collapsed 80 yards from the finishing post, ending the Queen Mother's hopes of winning the Grand National

The Queen leads in Carozza, Lester Piggott up, after winning the Oaks at Epsom in 1957

Previous page: The royal party at Epsom before the Derby

The Prince of Wales leading the field in a point-to-point in 1932

Monaveen had a colourful past having progressed from pulling an Irish milk float to the glory of carrying royal colours, and had once changed hands for £35. He had his first outing on October 10 at Fontwell Park and won with ease by fifteen lengths.

The fairy tale was to come to a tragic end. Monaveen had to be destroyed after breaking a leg at the water jump while lying second in the £2,000 Queen Elizabeth Chase at Hurst Park, at the beginning of December 1950. By winning £3,293, however, he had not only paid for himself, but had made a considerable profit for his owners. He was also the first horse for 235 years to run for a Queen of England, since the time of Queen Anne who founded Ascot Races in 1711 and whose horse won a race at York only a few days before her death.

Princess Elizabeth gave up as an owner for a while to concentrate on her young family and on doing up Clarence House, and

The Queen Mother congratulates Dumfermline after the Queen's filly had won the Oaks in Jubilee year

Opposite: The Queen Mother and Princess Margaret at Ascot in 1981

when she ascended to the throne in 1952 the additional responsibilities left her little time for horses and racing.

However, by 1954 the Queen was an owner again and, true to royal tradition, a successful one. Aureole became a firm favourite, winning the King George VI and Queen Elizabeth Stakes at Ascot worth £23,302 in 1954. By the time he retired to stud at Sandringham, where the Queen frequently went to talk to him in his stable, he had won £36,225.

That same year the Queen topped the owners' table with winnings of £62,211 collected from 30 races. The following year she won £47,000 and in 1959 £38,000. Her winnings from the first seven years as an owner averaged £32,000.

1960 was a disappointing year for the Queen, her winnings dropping to a mere £2,310 and the next few seasons saw a continuing decline in the Queen's success. In 1962 she added Captain Peter Hastings-Bass to her training strength. "My grandfather trained a steeplechasing winner for Her Majesty's grandfather – and I only hope I can do as well as my predecessors and colleagues," he said.

Prince Charles takes a tumble from Good Prospect at Sandown Park in March 1980

1965 saw an upturn in her fortunes. For the first time since 1900 when Diamond Jubilee won for the then Prince of Wales, the Eclipse Stakes at Sandown Park saw a royal winner, the Queen's four-year-old, Canisbay. By the end of the season Her Majesty had won more than £43,000 in stake money.

1974 was her best year when she won her first classic race for sixteen years with Highclere's victory in the One Thousand Guineas. The horse went on to win *Le Prix de Diana* – the French Oaks – rounding off her total winnings to nearly £140,000. Since then the Queen has won three more classics, the St Leger once and the Oaks twice, with her filly Dunfermline and she was voted Owner of the Year by the Racehorse Writers' Association in her Jubilee Year, 1977.

Although Pall Mall broke the Queen's classic 'duck' by winning the Two Thousand Guineas six years after Aureole won the Derby Trial at Lingfield in Coronation year, her racing manager Lord Porchester's vote for her best horses goes to Highclere and Dunfermline as fillies and to Aureole as the most successful colt.

In 1979, Prince Charles, speaking to the Iron and Steel Trades Confederation, said: "Whenever I back one of my mother's horses, it is always a total disaster. I keep well out of that and advise you to do the same thing." But for once the Prince had

The Prince of Wales well placed at Cheltenham

Opposite: Members of the royal family in the Winner's Enclosure at Ascot

given the wrong advice. Days later the Queen's horse Buttress romped home a 3 – 1 winner in the Queen's Vase at Royal Ascot, and she had a second winner in Expansive.

In 1980 the Queen had thirteen winners and in 1981, fourteen. The promising young filly Height of Fashion won a listed race at York in August and a group race at Doncaster in September.

The Queen Mother's success in the racing field is shown by her total of 335 winners to date. She was involved in one of the great mysteries in racing – the question of why her horse, Devon Loch, stopped only yards short of the winning post in the 1956 Grand National. Devon Loch, with two wins already under his belt, was a strongly fancied second favourite and was five or six lengths clear when he appeared to slip on the wet track and came to a standstill. Although her disappointment must have been acute, the Queen Mother had not one word of reproach for him. "You dear poor old boy," she said, patting his neck. There was no veterinary explanation for the extraordinary occurrence although the horse received ten months treatment for tendon trouble before being retired. The Queen Mother and Princess Margaret took a close interest in his recovery and visited him frequently.

In 1957 the Queen Mother won the Tote Investors Cup at

Prince Charles' debut as a steeplechase jockey at Sandown Park in March 1980

Newbury with Double Star and told the stewards afterwards that she had never won a cup before, adding: "I shall have to take it home to show Prince Charles".

The following year she was given the black gelding Bali Ha'i by the New Zealand Government and the horse won its first race the next spring, the Coombe Stakes at Sandown Park netting the Queen Mother £1,200 in prize money. He also won the Queen Alexandra Stakes before being sent back to New Zealand for retirement.

In 1961 the Queen Mother had the best season for twelve years and got her first hat trick. Three of her horses won successive races at Lingfield and she finished the season with twelve winners. The same year she gave one of her favourite steeplechasers Brig-o-Dee to the Metropolitan Police after he was found not to be suitable for the Queen on ceremonial occasions.

The next year the Queen Mother was top owner with nineteen winners, including Gay Record in the Hunter Handicap, and

The Queen with her trainer, Ian Balding, watching a string of racehorses returning from early morning exercise

collected £7,000 in stake money. The same year she also became the first member of the royal family to keep a horse in Ireland since King Edward VII. Her horse, Arch Point, entered for the Dublin Horse Show and this was the first time the royal family had exhibited.

In October 1964 the Queen Mother notched up her 100th winner with Gay Record's victory at Folkestone and a hat trick there meant she finished the season as leading owner with a total of 106 winners. "She was up and down like a two-year-old," said a friend. Her grandson Prince Andrew, then four but quite aware that this was Olympic year, asked if his granny would get a gold medal for her triumph.

The Queen Mother has lots of form books and supervises the buying of all her horses. She also takes a close personal interest in their training, going to watch them work out, armed with a pile of sugar and a bucket of carrots. She does not stand on ceremony as far as her horses are concerned and inspected Super Fox in the

Prince Charles with his grandmother, his aunt and his fiancee in the paddock at Sandown

Opposite: The Prince mounted on Good Prospect

front garden of her London home Clarence House. She found one horse, the famous The Rip, in a field behind the Red Cat pub in Norfolk.

So passionate is she about racing that in 1965 she had 'The Blower', a racecourse commentary service, installed in Clarence House. Through this service she receives the same information as betting shops about prices, jockey changes and weights.

When the Queen Mother had to go into hospital for an abdominal operation ITV specially taped a race at Sandown for her so she could see her horse Irish Rover run.

By the end of the 1967 season the Queen Mother had owned fifty-one horses and won 160 races worth £74,272. Two years later she got her 200th winner when Master Daniel won at Worcester. Her winnings were up to £95,000.

The Queen Mother has had her share of disasters. In May 1969 Chaser Woodman had a fatal fall at Newton Abbot and in 1970 Colonsay Isle and Playagain were destroyed within a week of each other. In March 1972 Capstan collapsed and died of a haemorrhage at Wye while leading the field and Game Spirit, winner eight times at Newbury, collapsed and died there in 1977.

But in these years the Queen Mother also had her triumphs. In November 1972 she reached the 250 winner mark with Chaou's

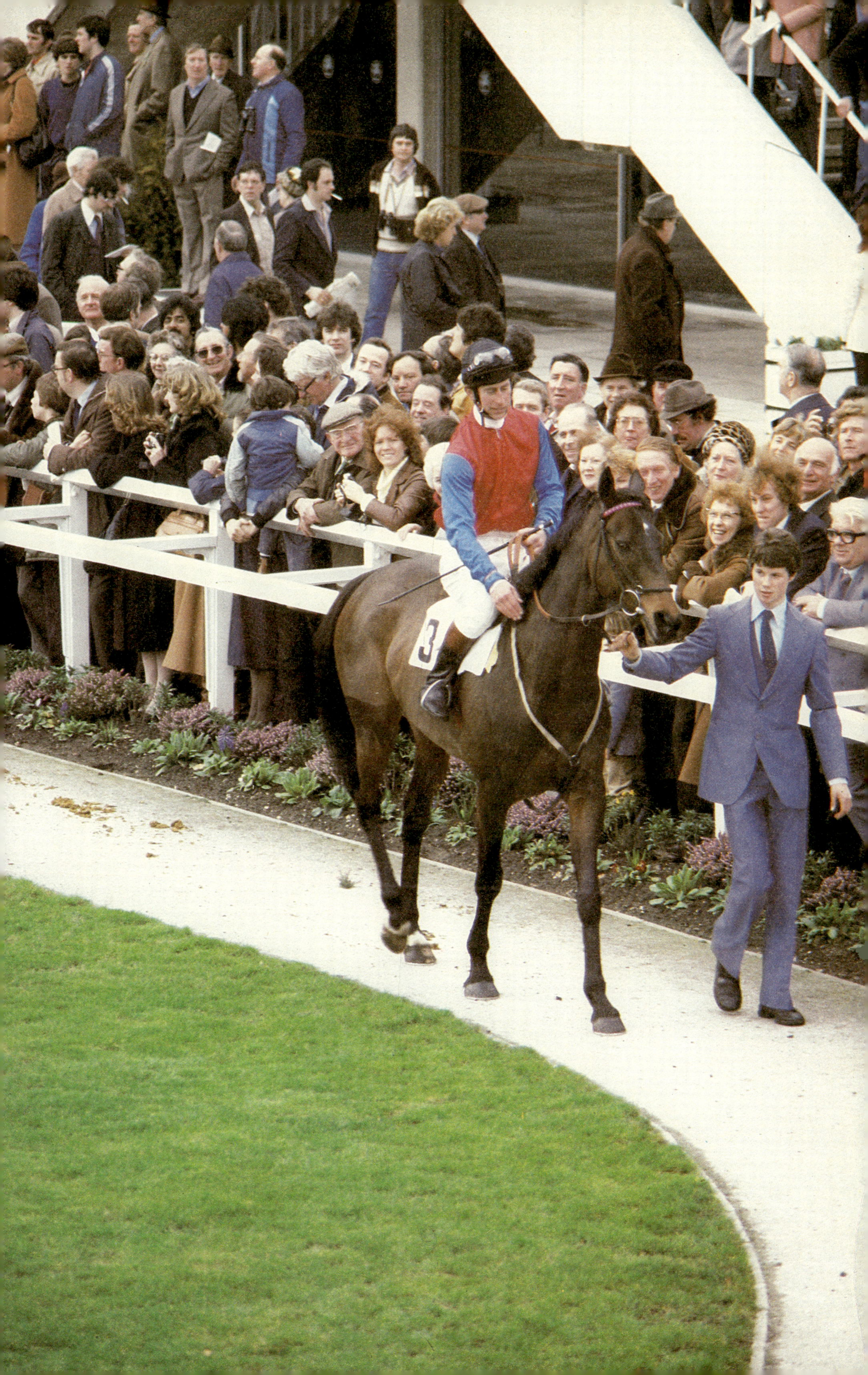

Lady Diana, as she was, strolls among racegoers at Ascot. The author is just behind her

victory at Fontwell Park and two years later Isle of Man and Present Arms won on their first outings. In 1975 Tammuz won the Schweppes Gold Trophy Handicap Hurdle at Newbury, worth nearly £10,000, the most valuable prize she has ever won. The following year she got her 300th winner with Sunnyboy at Ascot. In 1981 the Queen Mother had seven winners. Special Cargo did particularly well winning the Allenbrook Memorial Handicap Chase and the Kempton Novice Chase.

Like his great uncle the late Duke of Windsor, Prince Charles, although he likes racing, is keener on participating than watching Three years ago he announced his ambition to ride in the Grand National after tackling twenty-six tough jumps on a cross-country course in Cheshire. "Prince Charles was as nervous as a kitten before the start of the event but he enjoyed it very much and said he would like to tackle the National one day," a friend said afterwards.

Princess Alexandra and the future Princess of Wales in the carriage procession at Ascot

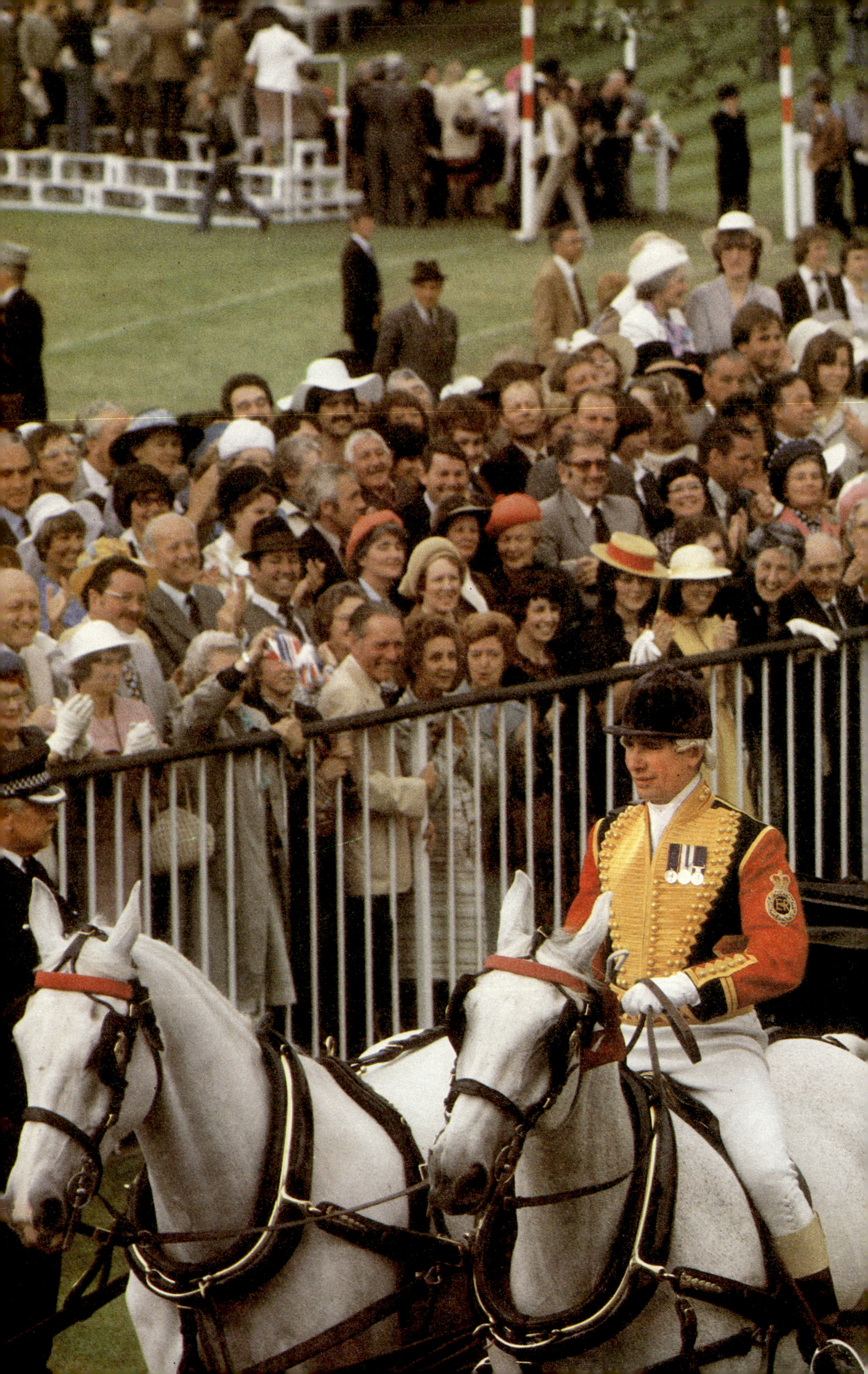

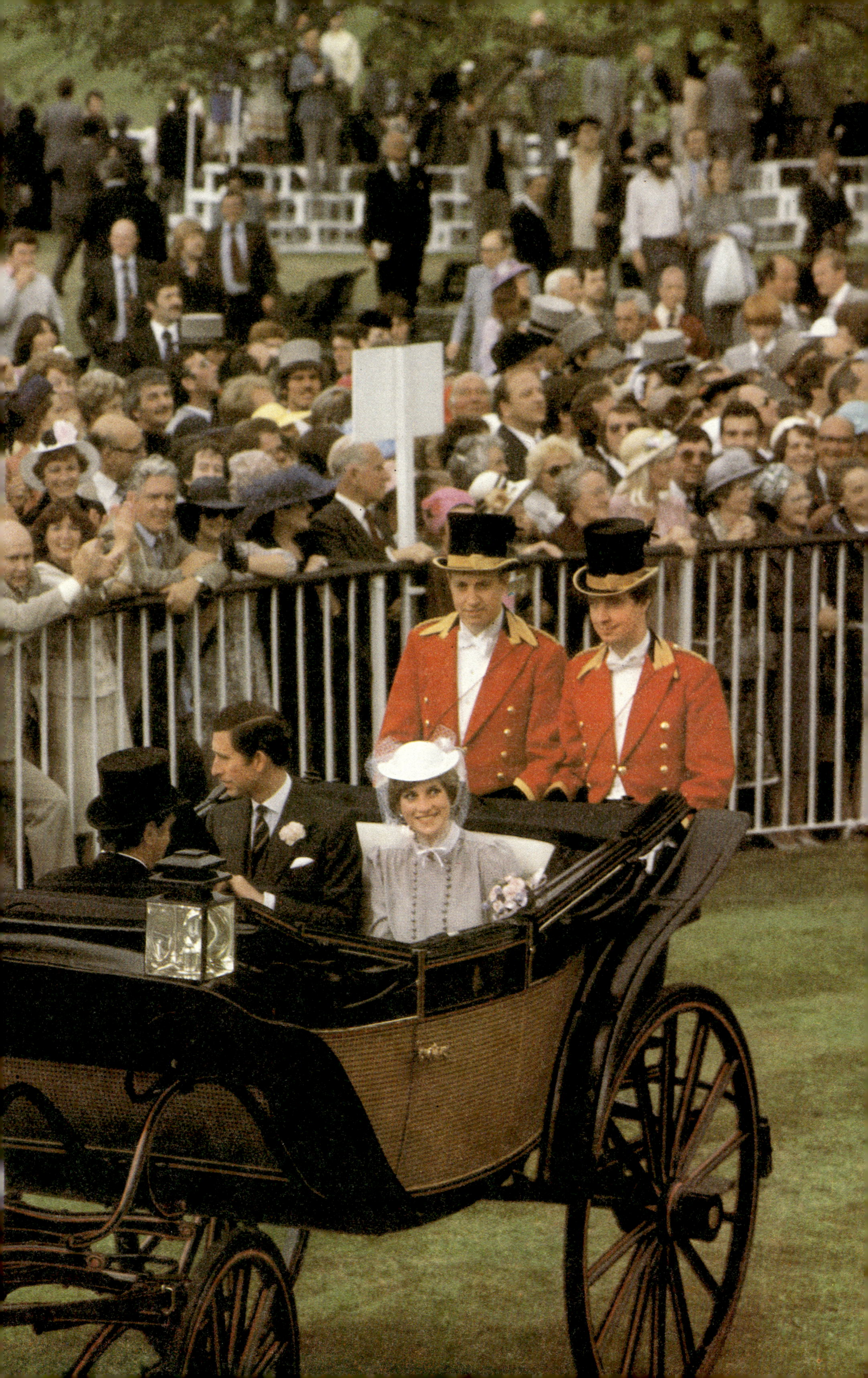

The same year he took part in racing at Upper Broughton in Nottinghamshire leading the Duke of Cornwall's Chasers. He fell twice and his team came second. Undeterred he was said to have "enjoyed it very much".

The following March he finished second in his first race on Long Wharf, in the Madhatters Private Stakes at Plumpton. A week later he was in the saddle again riding Sea Swell in the Duke of Gloucester's Memorial Trophy, but despite trying hard in his first race over the sticks, the Prince finished last of four.

The Prince also had his share of spills. He fell three quarters of a mile from the finish at Sandown in March 1981 and five days later he was again out of the saddle at the tenth fence at Cheltenham. As he was later told by President Ronald Reagan, "There are going to be times when you and the horse part company. It's no reflection on the horseman's ability or horsemanship".

In February 1981 tragedy struck when the Prince's £15,000 racehorse Allibar collapsed and died while out with the Prince on the Lambourn Downs. His bride-to-be Lady Diana Spencer was with him and the royal couple were naturally very distressed by the incident. However, shortly afterwards the Prince bought the steeplechaser Good Prospect for whom he paid £1,200, only to be unseated by the horse during a race at Sandown.

In May the Prince was in the saddle again riding the Queen Mother's eleven-year-old gelding Upton Grey at Newton Abbot in Devon. He finished ninth out of fourteen riders but it was later explained that the Prince had only taken part as it was his last chance of the season. The horse was known to hate soft ground and a friend said: "The Prince didn't really have a chance of winning – he just had the wrong horse." This was the Prince's sixth race in public. He has twice finished runner-up, first at Plumpton and later on Allibar when he raced at Ludlow.

But no doubt Prince Charles will be in the saddle before long hoping to gain his first victory.

Previous page: The colourful pageantry of the procession as the Prince and Princess of Wales drive through the golden gates into the Royal Enclosure at Ascot

In May 1924 the Prince of Wales and the Duke of York on opposite sides in a polo match at Ranelagh

POLO

FOR THOUSANDS of years polo has been the sport of kings. The game originated in Persia some 2,500 years ago and as it gained in popularity spread throughout Asia to China, Japan and India where it was discovered by English cavalry officers who brought it back to England.

One of the finest polo grounds ever built is still to be found at Isfahan. Its pitch, 300 yards long and 200 yards wide, with its stone goal posts eight yards apart would meet the needs of present day players.

In the 16th century the Mongolian Emperor Akbar decided to build a new city at Agra but it is said that he found the noise of construction so irritating that he ordered a city of pleasure to be built seven miles to the south. There he and a few chosen friends

Next page: Prince Charles represented England II against France on Imperial International Polo Day in 1979. His team won 5—2

43

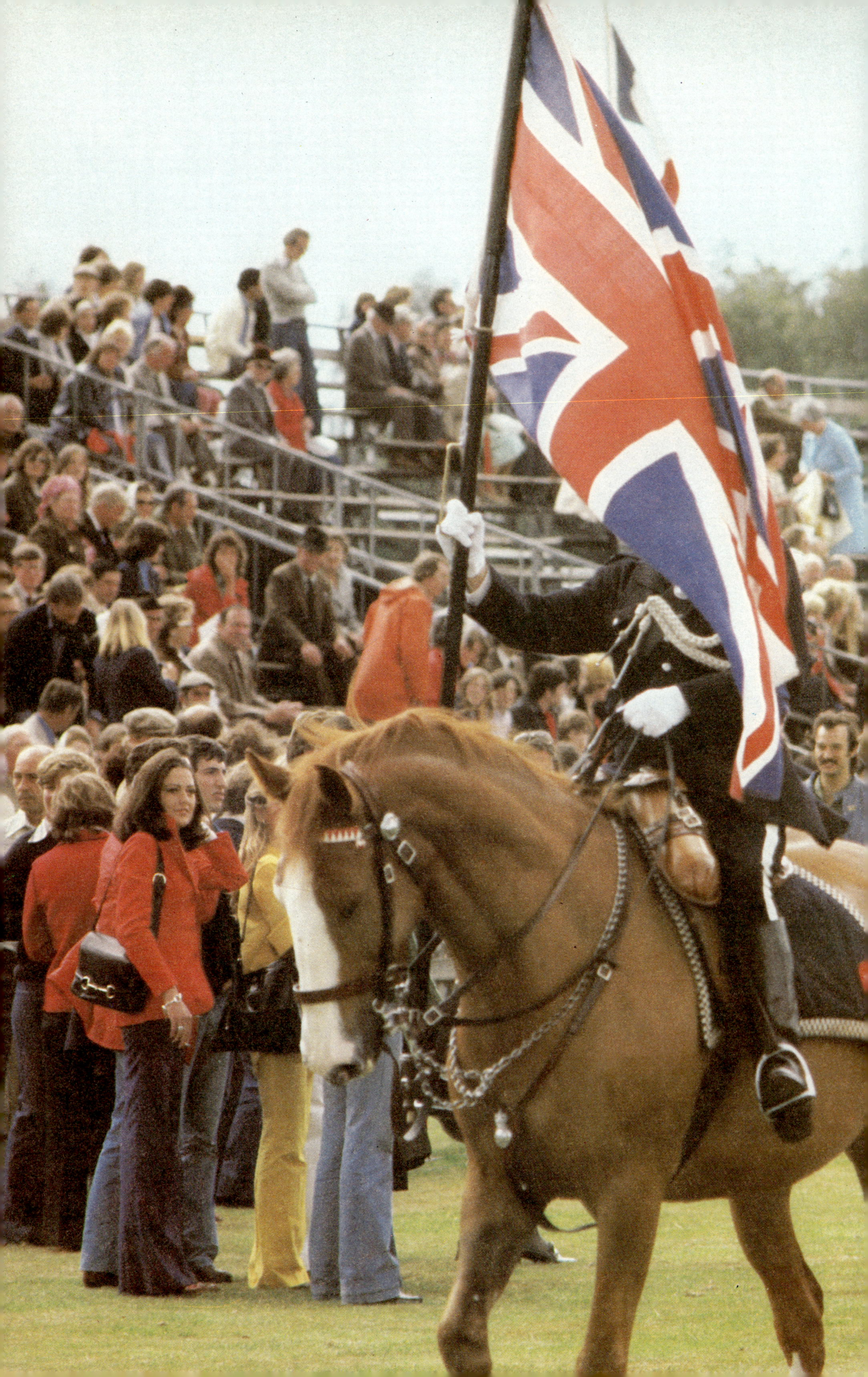

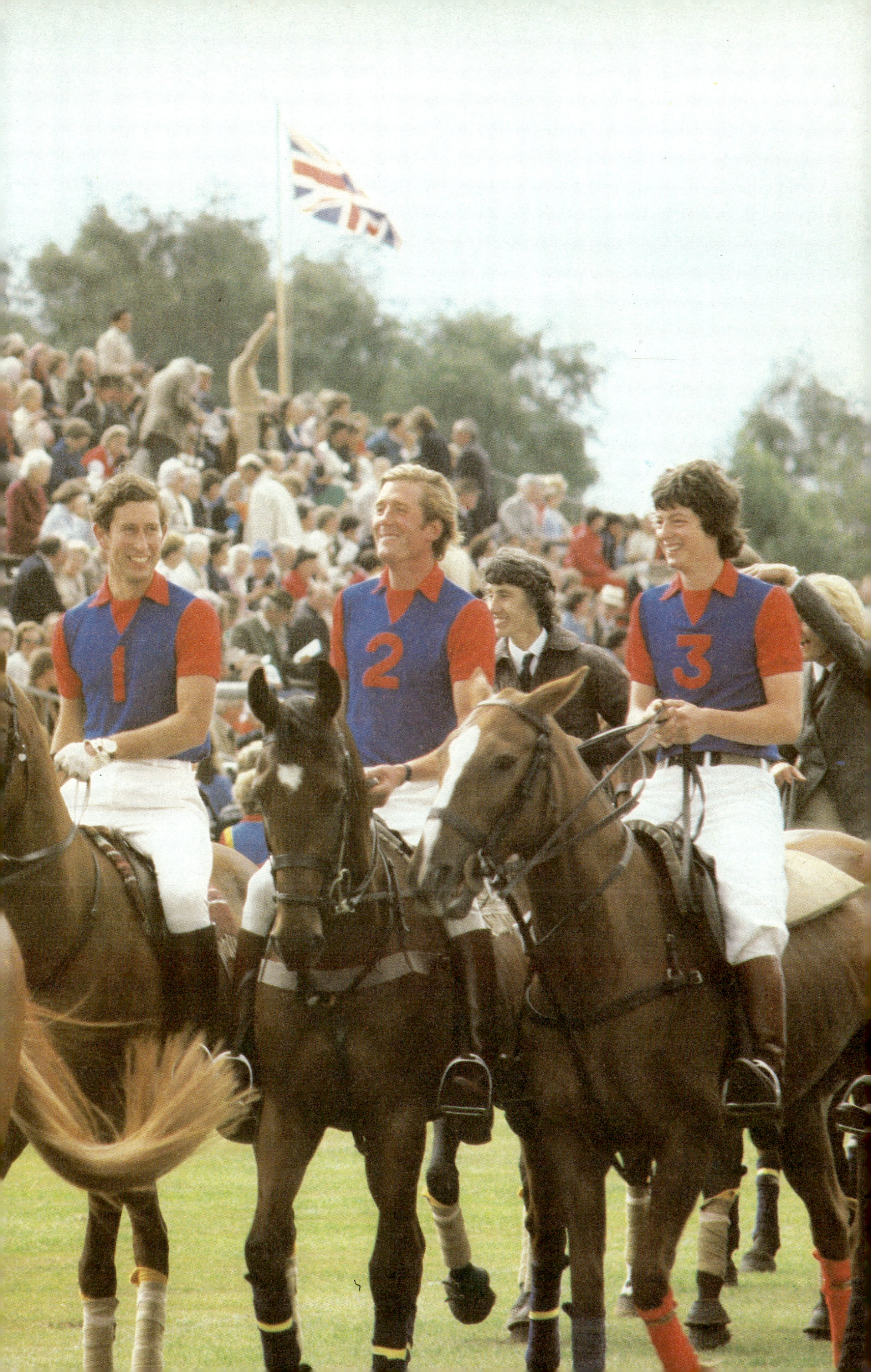
1
2
3

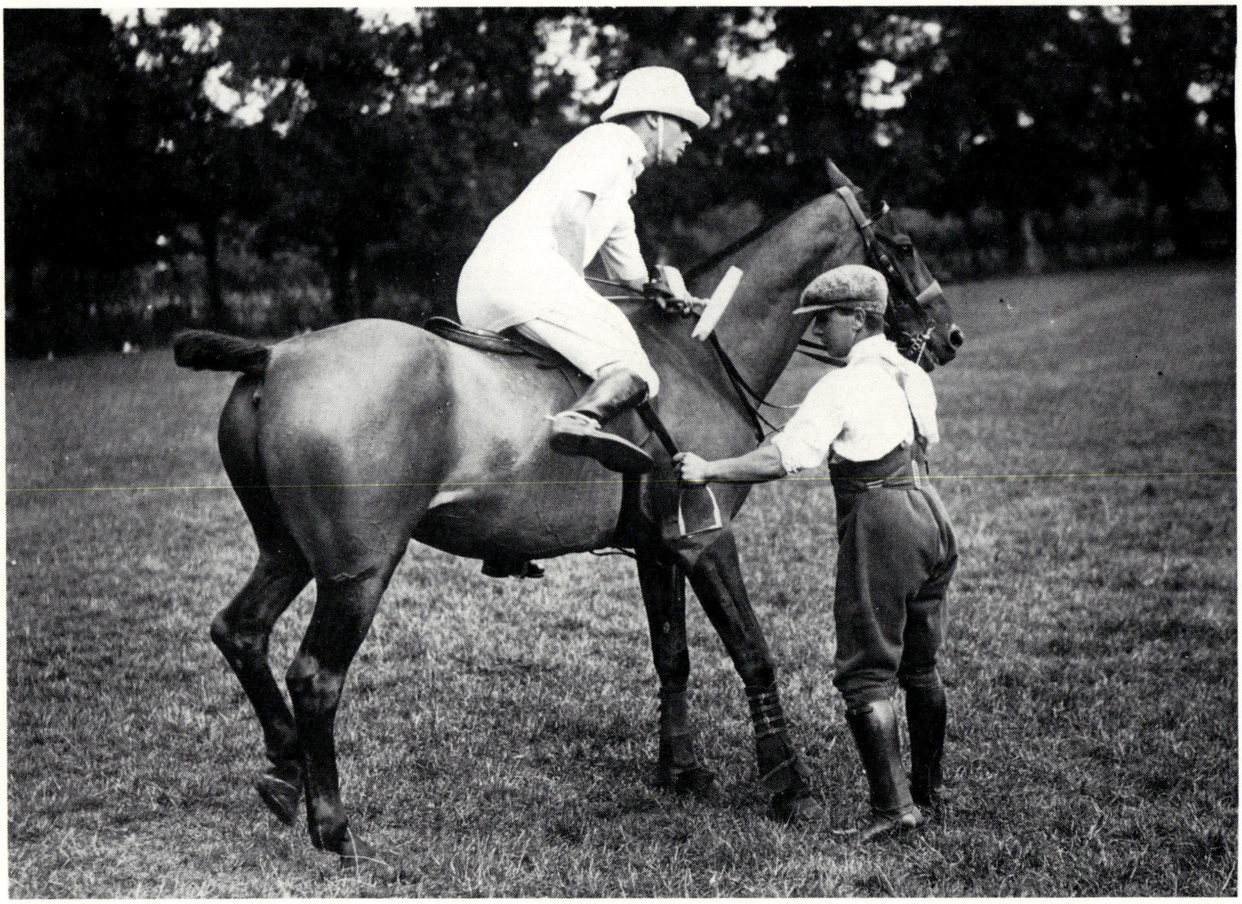

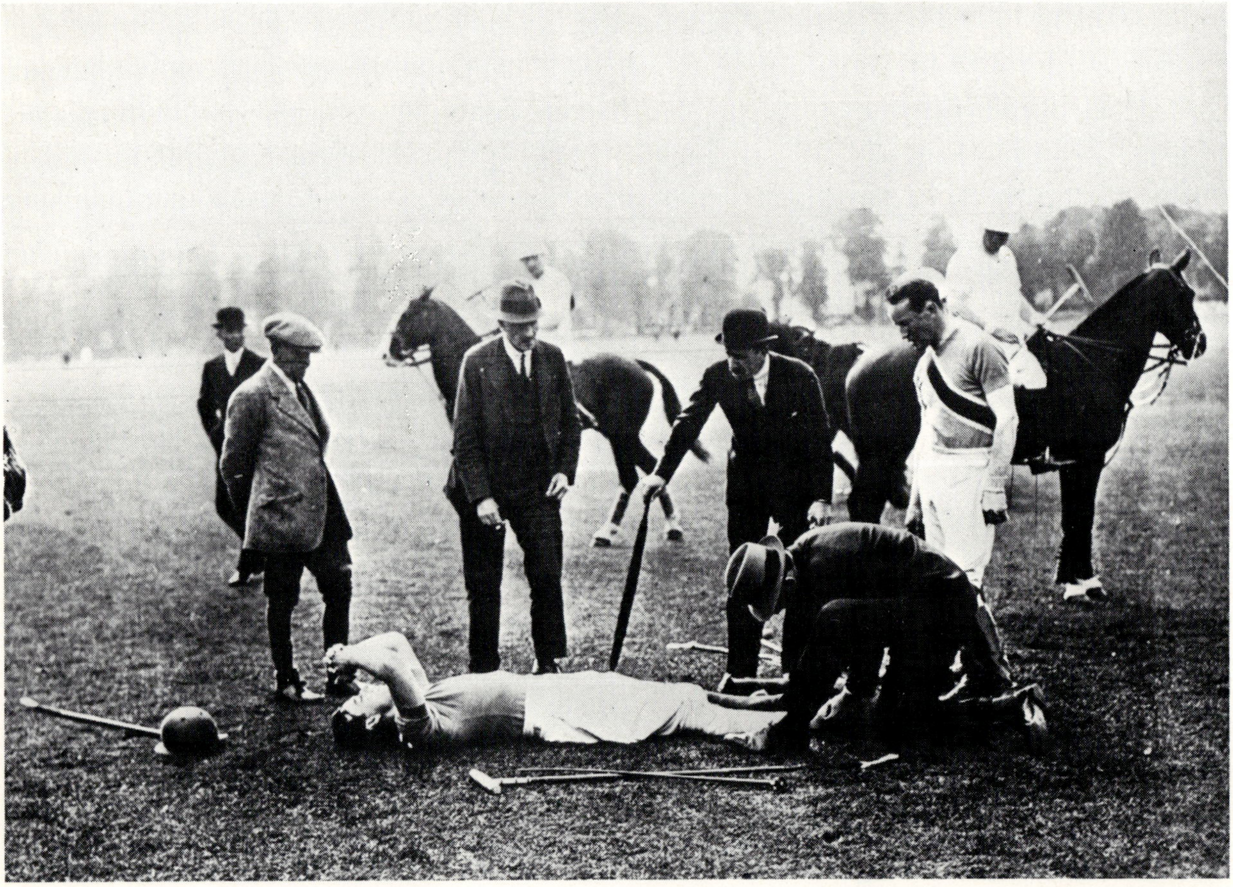

Far left: The Duke of York changes ponies during a polo match in 1924

An action shot of Lord Mountbatten playing at Roehampton in 1950

flew their birds of prey, raced their wild dogs and played polo. So fanatical was the emperor about the game that he invented a smouldering wooden ball so he could play under the stars. One of his team, who did not show proper enthusiasm for polo, was banished on a pilgrimage to Mecca.

In the early days of polo some players preferred to use the severed head of an enemy for a ball while others, with teams of forty a side, the body of a goat. The player carrying the goat's carcass had to gallop through the goal posts while the remaining seventy-nine players, from his own and the opposition's side, tried to stop him.

The aim of the game is, in some respects, unchanged today although time has moderated its more barbaric aspects and flaming polo balls have declined in popularity.

The English cavalry preferred a more controlled, though no less physical game, where two teams of not more than four players each, attempt to hit a white wooden ball through the opposition's goal posts. The first polo match to be played in England was

Bottom left: Lord Louis Mountbatten flattened after a fall at polo. The concerned-looking gentleman with the umbrella is King Alfonso of Spain

Prince Charles playing for a local army team in Sao Paulo, Brazil

between the 9th Lancers and the 10th Hussars and took place at Hounslow in 1871. History does not relate who won.

Since then the sport has spread to almost every country in the world gaining the greatest popularity in the Argentine and the United States of America. The number of registered players in Britain has risen from 320 to 722 in the last four years.

The late Earl Mountbatten of Burma, the last Viceroy of India, was one of the first members of the British royal family to take up the sport. He said that when he went to the subcontinent in 1921 with the then Prince of Wales, later King Edward VIII, he discovered the three loves of his life – India, his wife Edwina and polo. Polo was an expensive sport for a young naval officer and Lord Mountbatten had never had the opportunity to play in England. Furthermore, he later said: "I was never naturally good at it," and modestly claimed that he was not a good horseman nor had a good eye for ball games. What appealed to him about polo was the close parallels it had with a naval battle, and Lord Mountbatten became a master tactician, making cine films – another of his great enthusiasms – of his team the Blue Jackets, and analysing them at length afterwards. Some unkind people likened him to a Prussian officer on the field.

The Earl played wherever and whenever he could both at home

A brilliant action shot of Prince Charles playing full back

and abroad and wrote what is still the definitive book on how to play the game, *An Introduction to Polo*, under the pseudonym Marco. It was his love of the game that first persuaded his nephew the Duke of Edinburgh and late his great nephew the Prince of Wales to take up the game and even in the last years of his life, he was a frequent and critical spectator.

Despite Lord Mountbatten's enthusiasm for polo, the Duke of Edinburgh came to the game late. He was twenty-eight and serving in the Royal Navy in Malta when he first picked up a polo stick, but once bitten by the polo bug there was no stopping him. With his usual energy and thoroughness he threw his heart into the game, practising whenever public duties allowed him a spare minute. He played for numerous sides, often at Cowdray Park, and by 1955 he was ready to captain his own team. He was one of the founder members of the Windsor Park side and was soon arousing the wrath of the Free Church of Scotland for playing polo on the sabbath.

One of the early team members was Major Ronald Ferguson, now the unofficial master of polo to the Prince of Wales. He remembers the Duke of Edinburgh as a very hard player, always in the centre of the action, taking his fair share of knocks. Although the Duke became one of the best players in Britain,

The Duke of Edinburgh at Cowdray Park in 1952

Top right: The Duke receives the Cicero Cup from Mrs Rex Benson

Bottom right: The Duke took to umpiring when he gave up playing

with a handicap of five, Major Ferguson believes he could have gone higher: "Unlike the professional players Prince Philip could not play all year round. He could not practise as much because of his other duties and he could not play as often. Prince Charles suffers from the same thing."

The Queen with her young children Prince Charles and Princess Anne frequently used to turn up to see the Duke play at Smith's Lawn in Windsor Great Park. A favourite treat for the children was to be allowed to give sugar lumps to the polo ponies – a habit which Prince Charles still indulges to this day.

So engrossed was the Duke in the game that he once travelled 640 miles in a day by air, sea and road from Scotland and back to

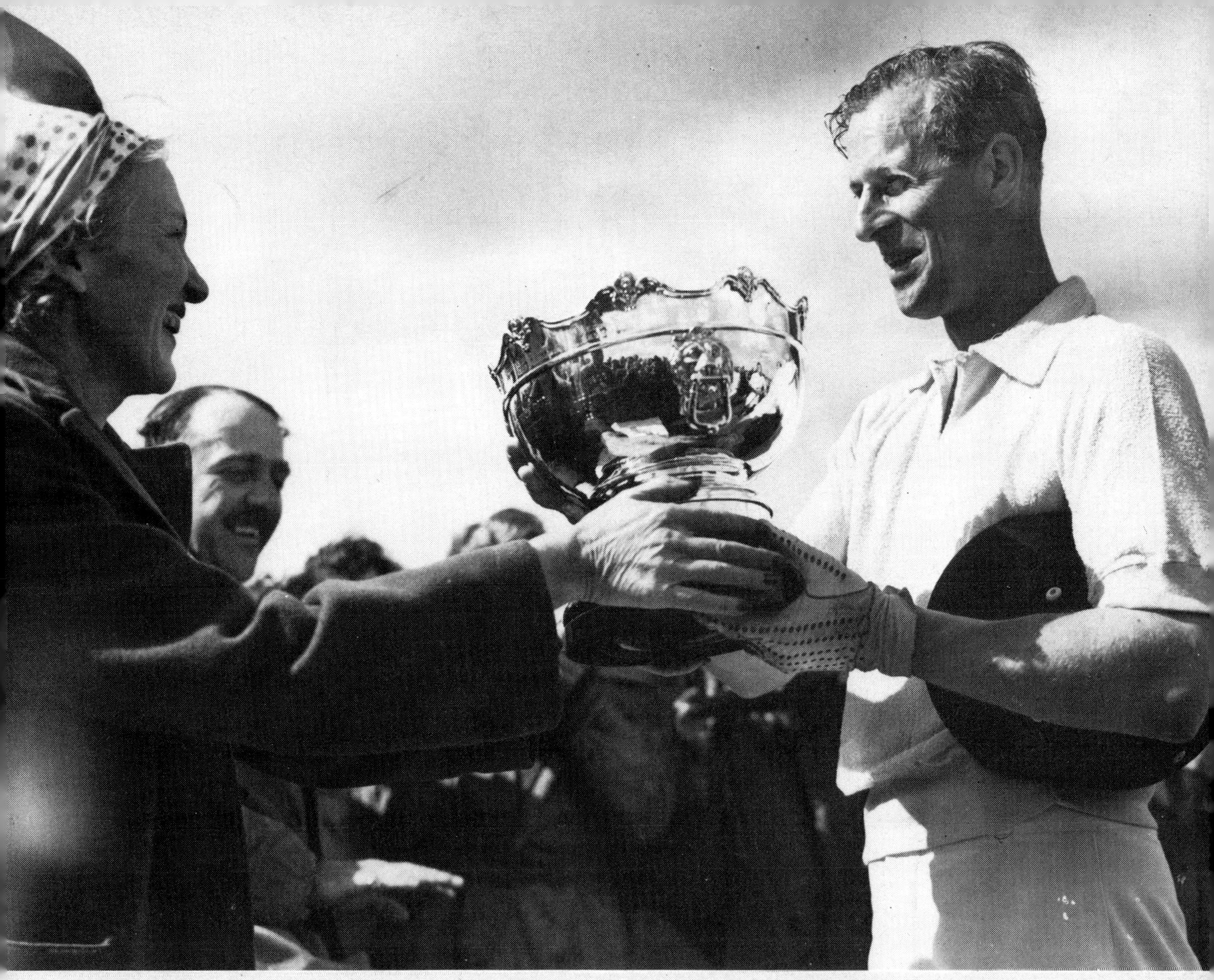

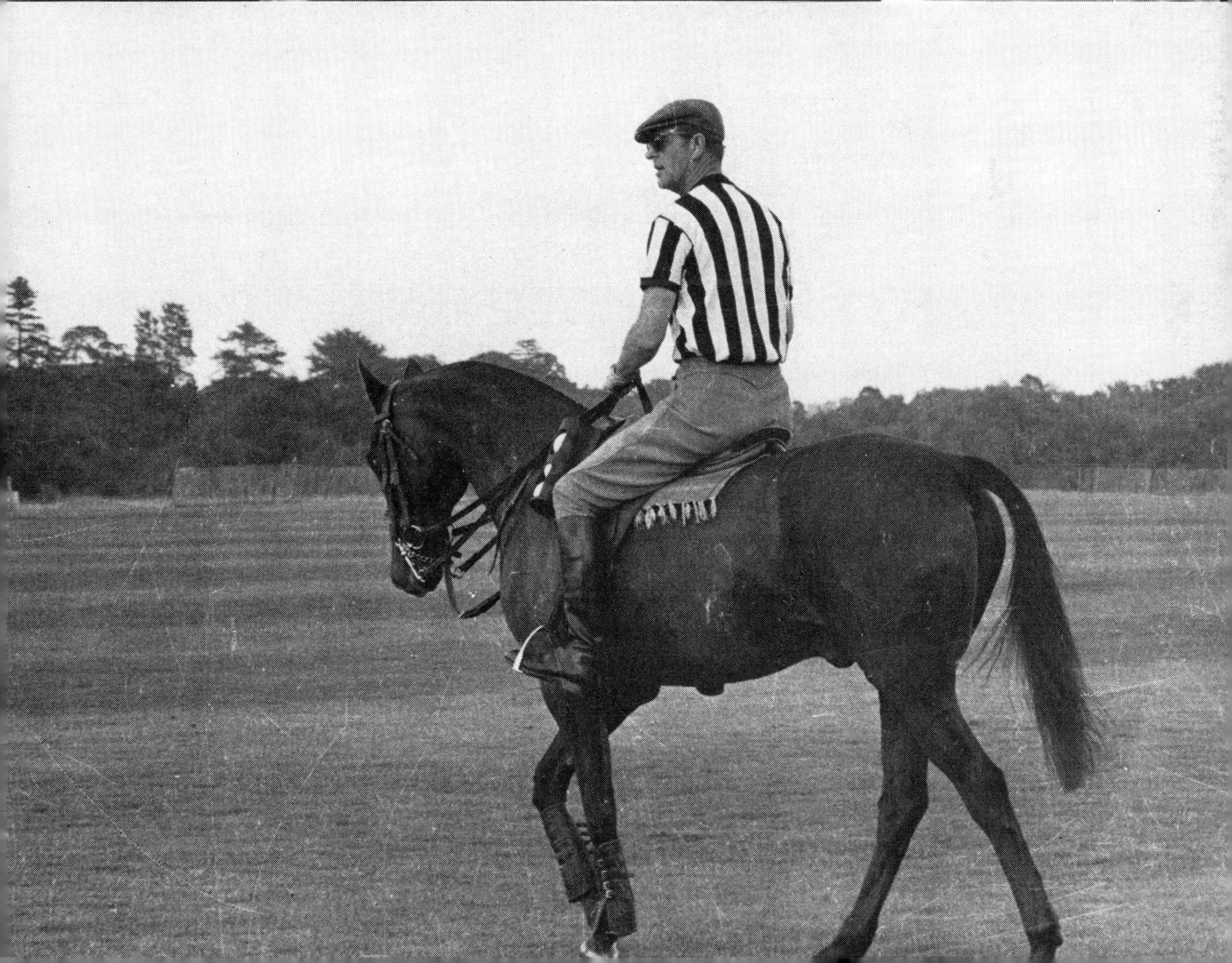

Prince Charles sometimes takes to the referee's stripes and whistle

take part in the 1958 final of the Royal Windsor Cup. As if to reward his trouble, his Windsor Park team won and he scored two goals.

It was about this time that the Duke of Edinburgh introduced his eldest son to polo, and many happy afternoons were spent on the tennis courts of Home Park, Windsor, where a polo pitch was laid out. Prince Charles and Princess Anne, armed with miniature polo sticks, would ride their bicycles and attempt to shoot tennis balls through a goal. The Duke, who was often heard to complain that he was more exhausted after a children's match than after a real game of polo, acted as goalkeeper. As a fellow enthusiast was heard to remark at the time: "It will not be Prince Philip's fault if Prince Charles doesn't turn out to be a champion player."

The Duke himself did not fall far short of the title. That same year he was the third highest handicapped Englishman and three years later, after an exhibition match at Lahore in India, he was judged best player and won a polo pony. The Queen was there to make the presentation. Such a high handicap was not easily won. Polo is a rough sport and being a high goal scorer, the Duke was always in the thick of the action. During the next ten years the Duke fell many times, usually emerging bruised but otherwise

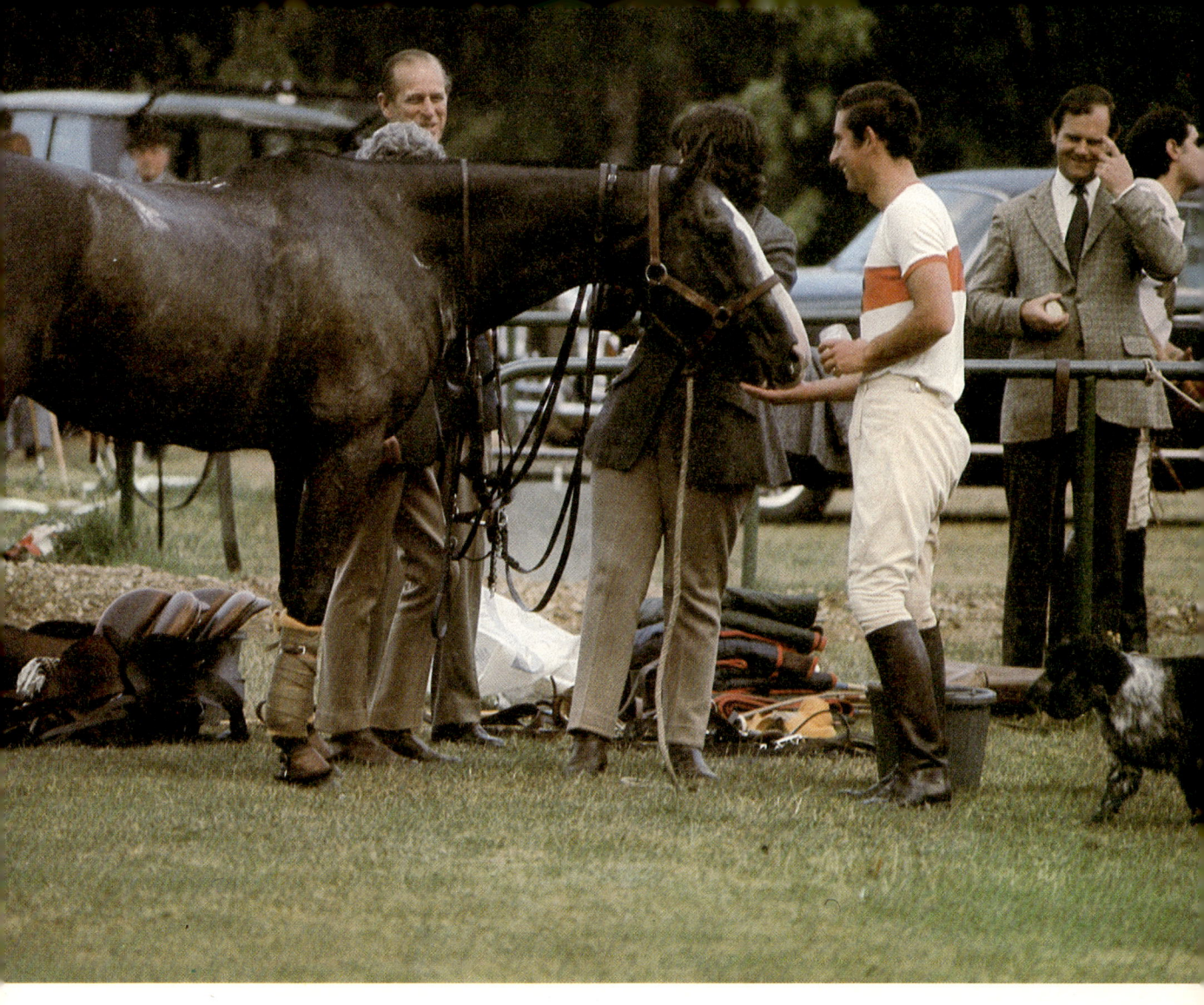

Ever fond of his ponies, the Prince always carries sugar in his pocket

unhurt. However, he did manage to break an ankle, although he continued to play for a further half hour after the accident, and in other encounters strained the ligaments in both shoulders and gashed his arm so badly that it needed three stitches.

Yet it was all worthwhile, for in the summer polo was the Duke's greatest relaxation. On the field he was treated like any other player and protocol thrown to the winds. He was shouted at just like any one of his team mates. The only concession made to his royal status was that the word 'Sir' would be tacked onto the end of every rocket. "Polo was one of his great joys. One could almost see the steam coming out of him on a Saturday after the frustrations of a week of public engagements," said Major Ferguson. Sadly for such an athletic and fit man, when the Duke of Edinburgh was fifty, Buckingham Palace announced that he was giving up the game because of attacks of synovitis, inflamed membranes, in his right wrist. He later confessed that he had used the controversial drug commonly known as bute to prolong his playing career. The Palace spokesman said, "He will continue his interest with occasional appearances as an umpire". However, this was not to be. Ever resourceful, the Duke had found a new passion – carriage driving.

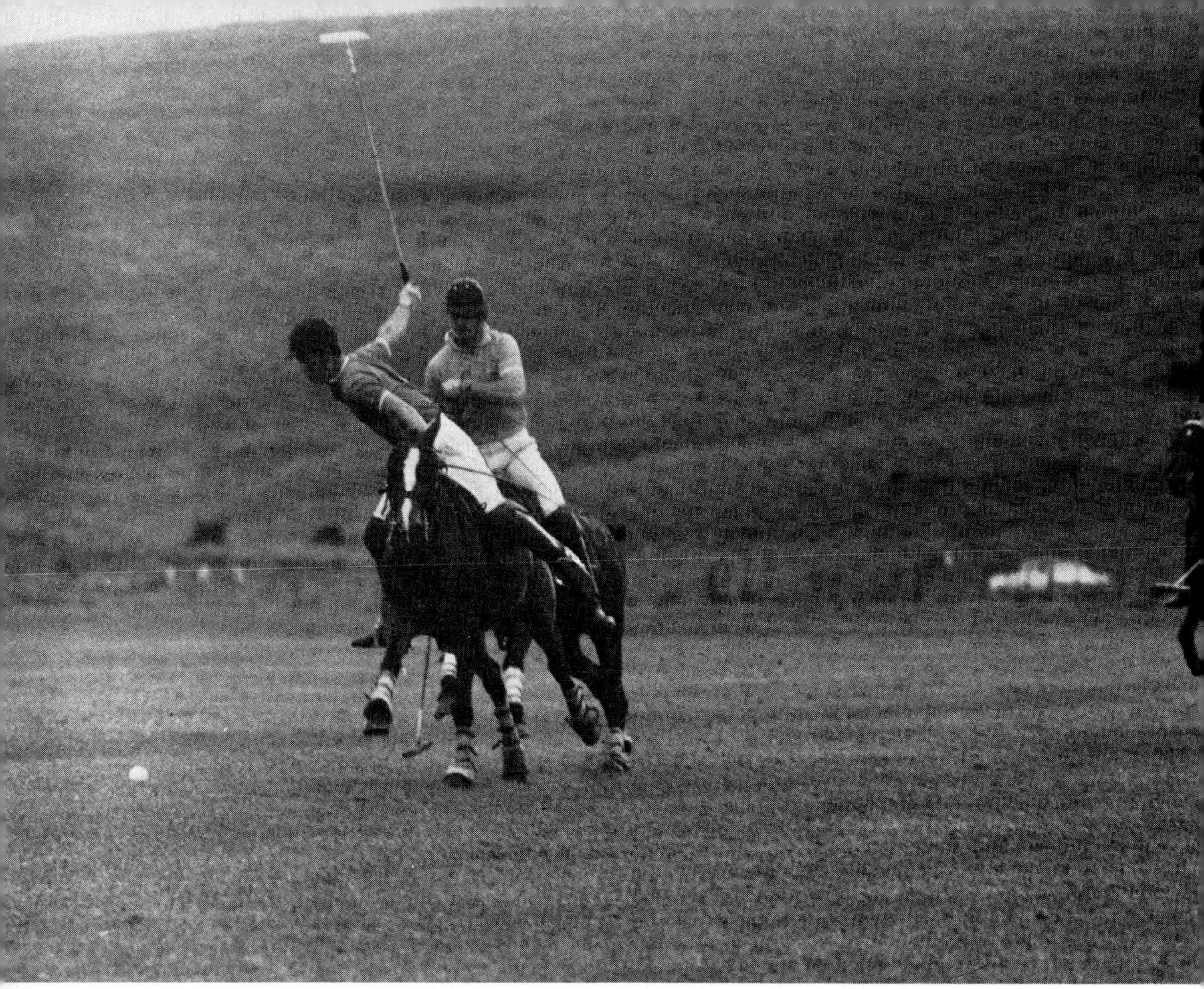

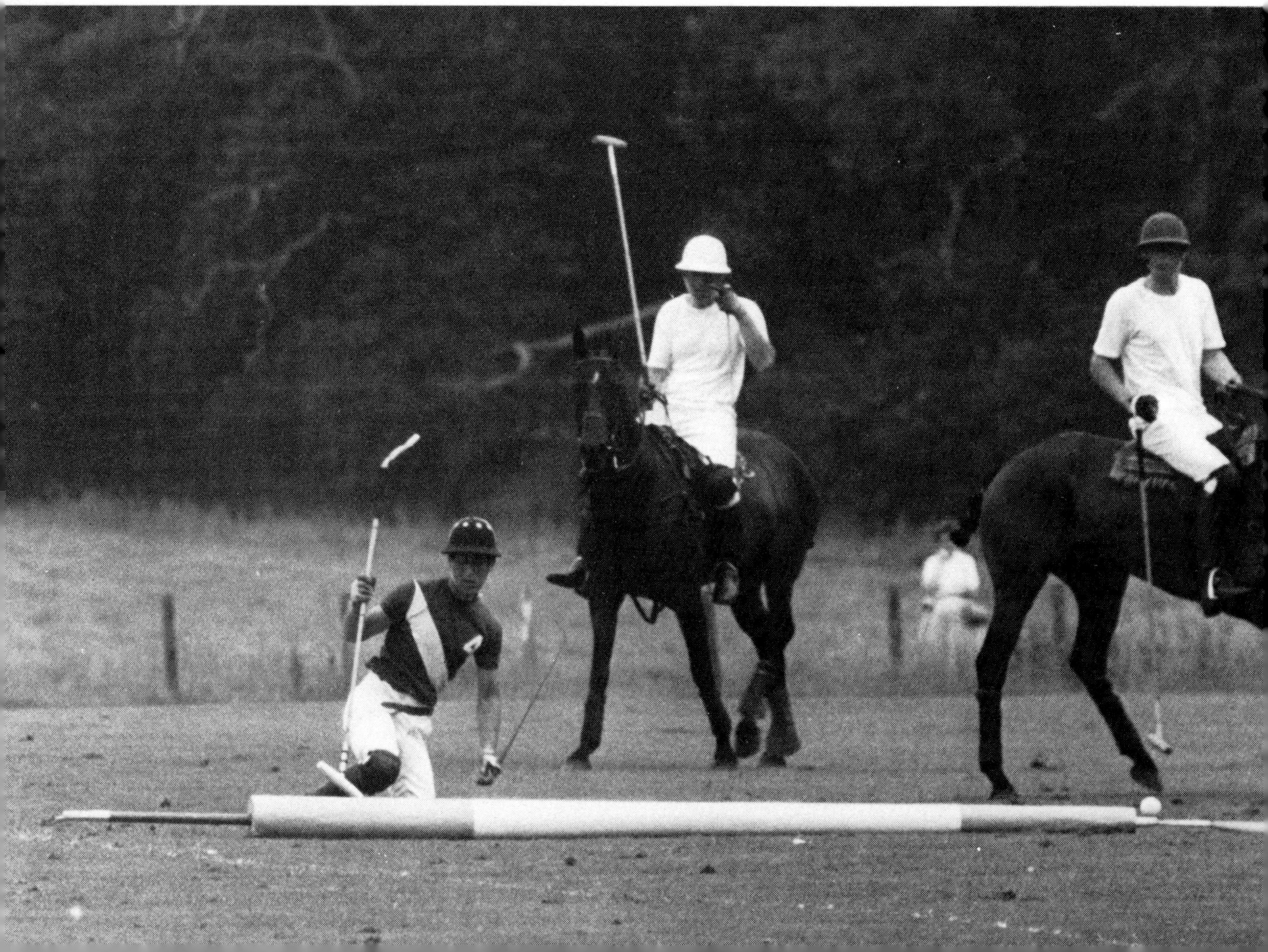

Meanwhile there were other royal players to take his place. Prince Charles, encouraged and coached by his father, had become a promising player while his cousin Prince William of Gloucester had also taken up the sport.

Prince Charles following in the Duke's footsteps, went on to play for England, but Prince William of Gloucester died tragically in a flying accident before he had got past the beginner stage.

Prince Charles played his first real game of polo at fifteen when he turned out in a team, captained by his father, against the Household Brigade on the private polo ground in Windsor Great Park. He already showed promise although the Duke is said to have laughed at him when he missed the ball. The following year he played in public for the first time, watched by the Queen and Princess Anne, who acted as his groom. In the match against the Household Brigade Polo Club he was said to have played 'quite well', hitting the ball accurately and never shirking going into an opponent. A week later he scored two goals in his first competitive match when his team Rangers beat Blacknest in the first round of the Chairman's Cup. "Prince Charles put up a fine performance against seasoned players," said an official.

1966 found Prince Charles in Australia where he captained his

In his last game as a bachelor, Prince Charles played for England II against Spain in the Imperial International Jubilee Cup. His team won and received medallions from the Queen

Top left: A fine shot of the Prince at full gallop in Australia

Far left: The Prince takes a spill after colliding with the goal post

The leading lady polo player, Claire Tomlinson was in the team playing against Prince Charles. On the left she receives her prize and on the right the two teams line up with the Queen

polo team to victory in Southern Victoria, scoring two goals. After the match John Lithgow, president of the Yarra Glen-Lulydale Club, said: "Prince Charles is an extremely good horseman and has a keen eye when it comes to hitting the ball. In a couple of years he will be a jolly good player." His words were prophetic and in the following year the Prince was said to have performed like a veteran when he played for the first time with his father in the Combermere Cup, scoring the fourth of six goals. His team went on to win the cup and the Duke of Edinburgh introduced his son to the Queen, who was presenting the prizes, with these words: "This is one of my team-mates whom I believe you know." The win got him his first prize for polo, a car compass. Later in the season Prince Charles scored the winning goal for Windsor in the final chukker of the Junior Counties Polo

Championship at Little Budworth in Cheshire. In November his handicap rose from minus one to zero.

While he was at Cambridge the Prince continued to play polo, getting his half-blue in his first year, but unfortunately the university lost both matches against Oxford during his time there.

By 1970 the Prince's handicap had risen to two and the following year he caused a stir by riding a pony named Christine Keeler while playing for the Nairobi Polo Club 'A' team. He scored three goals in two polo matches and helped his side win the tournament despite galloping into a goal post and bruising his wrist and hand. By now his string of polo ponies, kept in the Royal Mews, had grown to five.

In 1972, one of his best years, he captained the first Royal Navy side to play at Smith's Lawn for ten years and put in his best

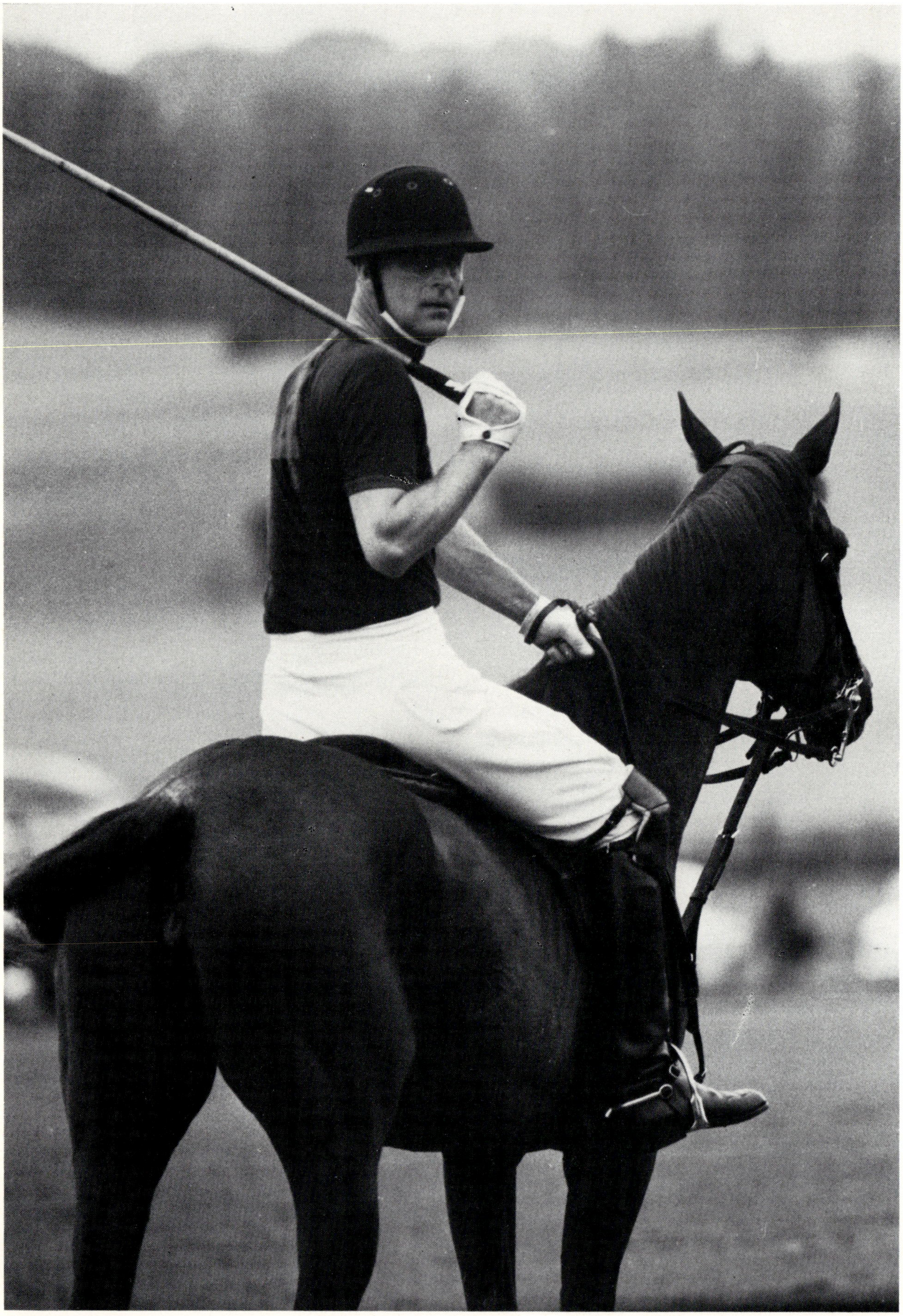

Lord Mountbatten was a great influence on Prince Charles. Here they share a joke at Smith's Lawn

performance ever, scoring six goals against a Blues and Royals team, who were beaten 10 – 0.

Later in the season he played in the Young England side in his first international match. The Fleet Air Arm, to whom he had presented the gun carriage trophy at the Royal Tournament, turned up to cheer him but despite their encouragement and his goal, his team went down 5 – 4 to Young America.

In the next few years Prince Charles had little chance to play much polo so taken up was he with his duties in the Royal Navy, and at the end of the 1973 season his handicap went down to three and his string of polo ponies down to two. Major Ferguson, a former Lifeguard, was appointed unofficial master of polo but by the end of the following season the Prince's handicap had dropped to two. "Prince Charles didn't play very often or very well this year and he did not have time to practise," said Major Ferguson.

Despite this setback 1975 found Prince Charles playing polo in India where he scored a goal from eighty yards which was said to be worthy of an eight handicapper. His team the Plumed Coronets beat the Ashoka Lions 9 – 6 and the Prince scored two goals. As the Prince approached his thirtieth birthday, a good age, he had once rather foolishly said, to get married, a stream of

Opposite: Prince Philip towards the end of his polo playing days

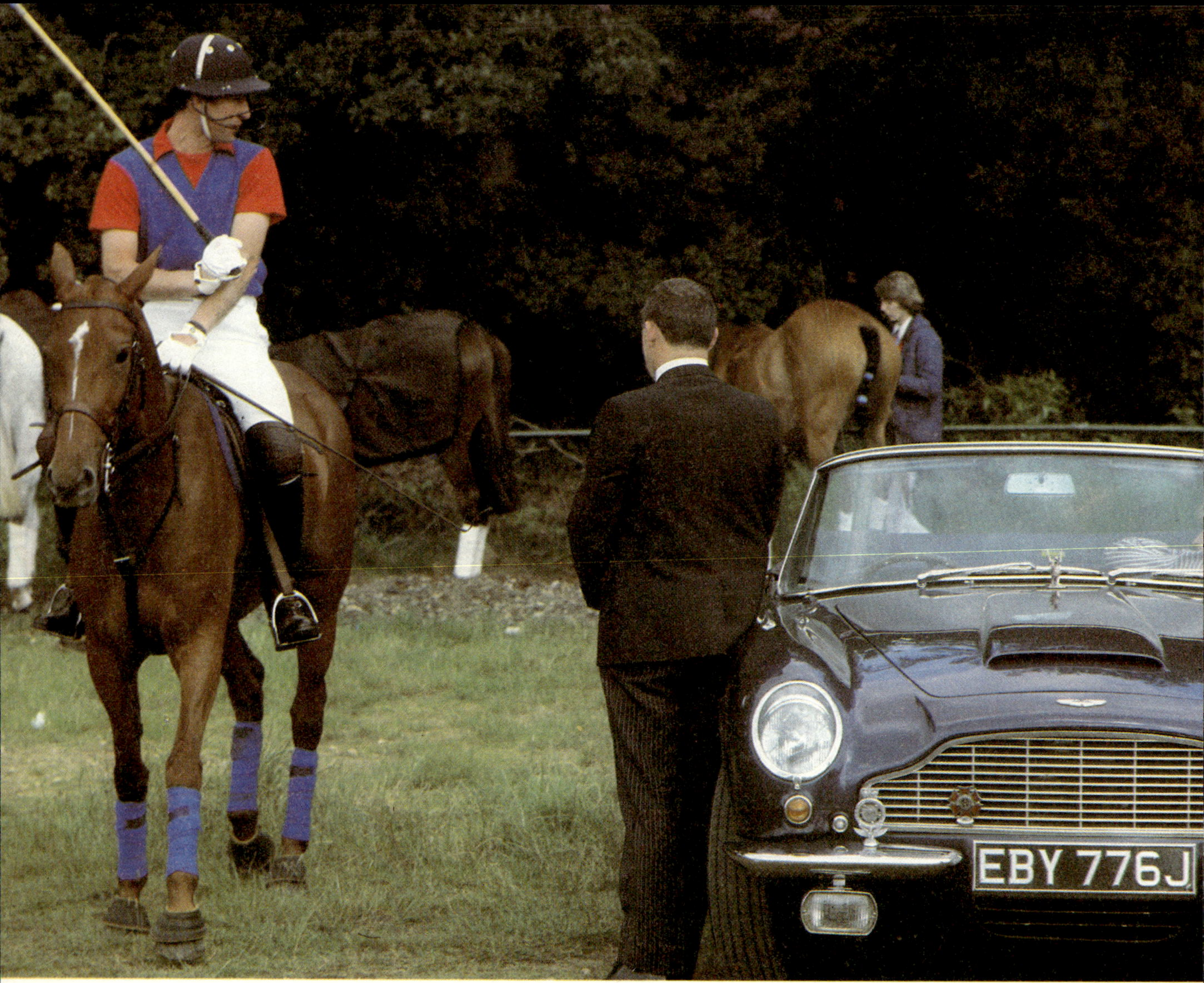
EBY 776J

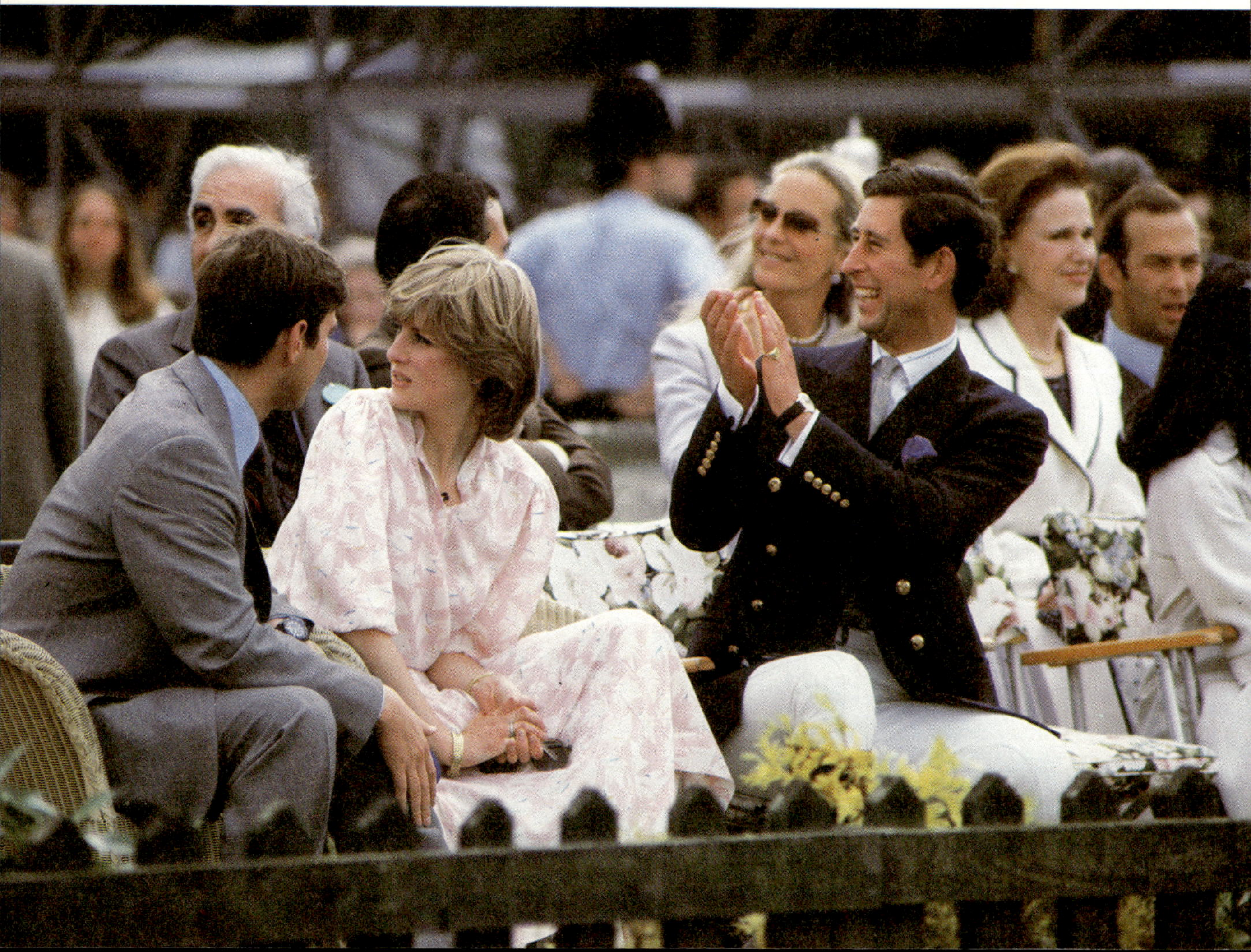

Prince Charles, wearing the English Rose, relaxes before a vigorous chukker

pretty girls were tipped as his bride to be. Many came to watch him play polo including Lady Sarah Spencer, the sister of the Princess of Wales.

His thirtieth year was an unhappy one as far as polo was concerned. He was thrown from his polo pony twice in five minutes in the first round of the Warwickshire Cup at Cirencester and later in the season a vet had to shoot his pony Norena after it fractured its pelvis during a Gold Cup match.

However, in the following year the Prince's handicap was back to four and he was saying of the game of polo: "I feel sheer terror but I also enjoy it tremendously." Thanks to the coaching of Australian ten-handicapped Sinclair Hill, who walked up to the Prince at Smith's Lawn and offered to help him with his game, Prince Charles had become an accomplished player. Mr Hill described the Prince as 'fearless' and his technique almost 'without fault' while Prince Charles was confidently predicting that he would go on playing polo until he was at least fifty. "You should never go on until you become a bore, getting in everyone's way and falling off. That's when your bones get broken because they get more brittle. I shall go on as long as I still bounce when I fall off – which I think I still do."

Top left: Prince Charles with his detective and his fiancee before a game of polo

Bottom left: A jovial moment in the royal box at Smith's Lawn

61

Last year the Prince played frequently in Britain as well as in India and once too often in Palm Beach, Florida, where he collapsed with the heat. "I thought I was going to die," he told an aide. Such commitment may be one reason why Major Ferguson feels the Prince's game can only improve. "I think he will go from strength to strength. I think his handicap will go as high as his father's but I would be surprised if it went above five because Prince Charles can't go abroad to play in the winter like some others and does not have as much time to practise."

Major Ferguson feels that the Prince's other riding activities like hunting and racing have made him "a more complete horseman which has obviously improved his game tremendously," added to which "he's got talent, he's got guts and he's got the drive to make a fine player." This year the Prince has lived up to this accolade playing in Australia and New Zealand as well as captaining the England II side. He even played both days of the weekend before his wedding, when England beat Spain 10 – 5 at the Imperial International Polo meeting.

Prince Charles has constantly denied that his bride the Princess of Wales hates polo and Major Ferguson confidently predicts that the Prince will be back in the saddle next season. "I am sure when all the fuss has died down the Princess will be there to watch him with the rest of the family," he said.

Prince Philip makes a splash at Windsor, driving the Queen's team of Cleveland Bays

CARRIAGE DRIVING

WHEN THE Duke of Edinburgh was forced to give up playing polo because of inflamed membranes in his right wrist he immediately found the new sport of carriage driving had one great advantage. This classical manner of travel relies on the left hand for its skills.

By the spring of 1972 the Duke was spending his every spare minute at Windsor Castle practising with a pair of horses under the expert eye of the Crown Equerry, Sir John Miller.

At the Royal Windsor Horse Show in May that year the Duke took the role of referee for the nineteen and a half mile marathon in the Barclays Bank International Driving Grand Prix, riding with the Hungarian team. He no doubt picked up some useful tips as he sat beside the driver, with stop-watch in hand, making sure there were no infringements of the rules. The Queen's team of four greys, driven by Sir John, came second.

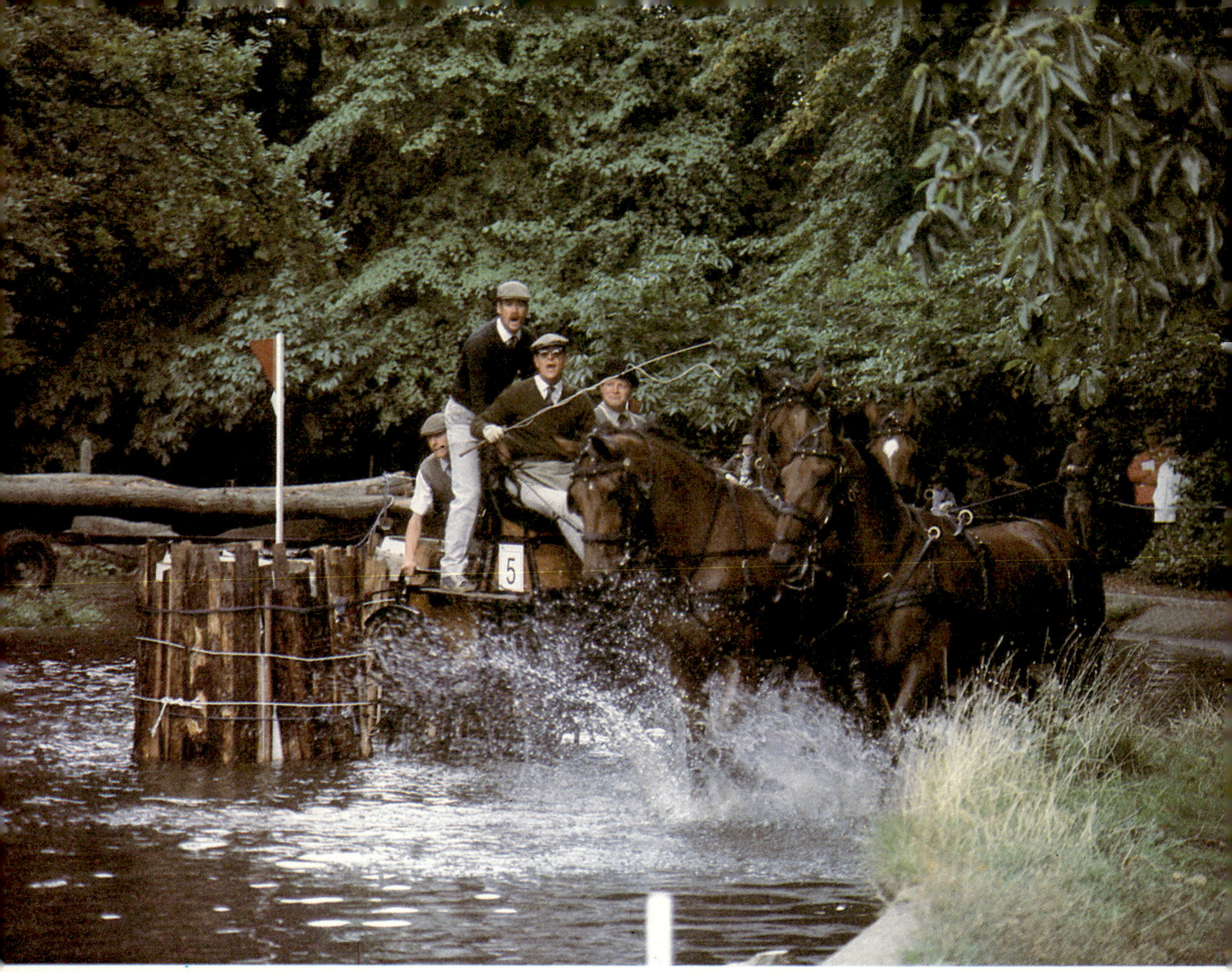
5

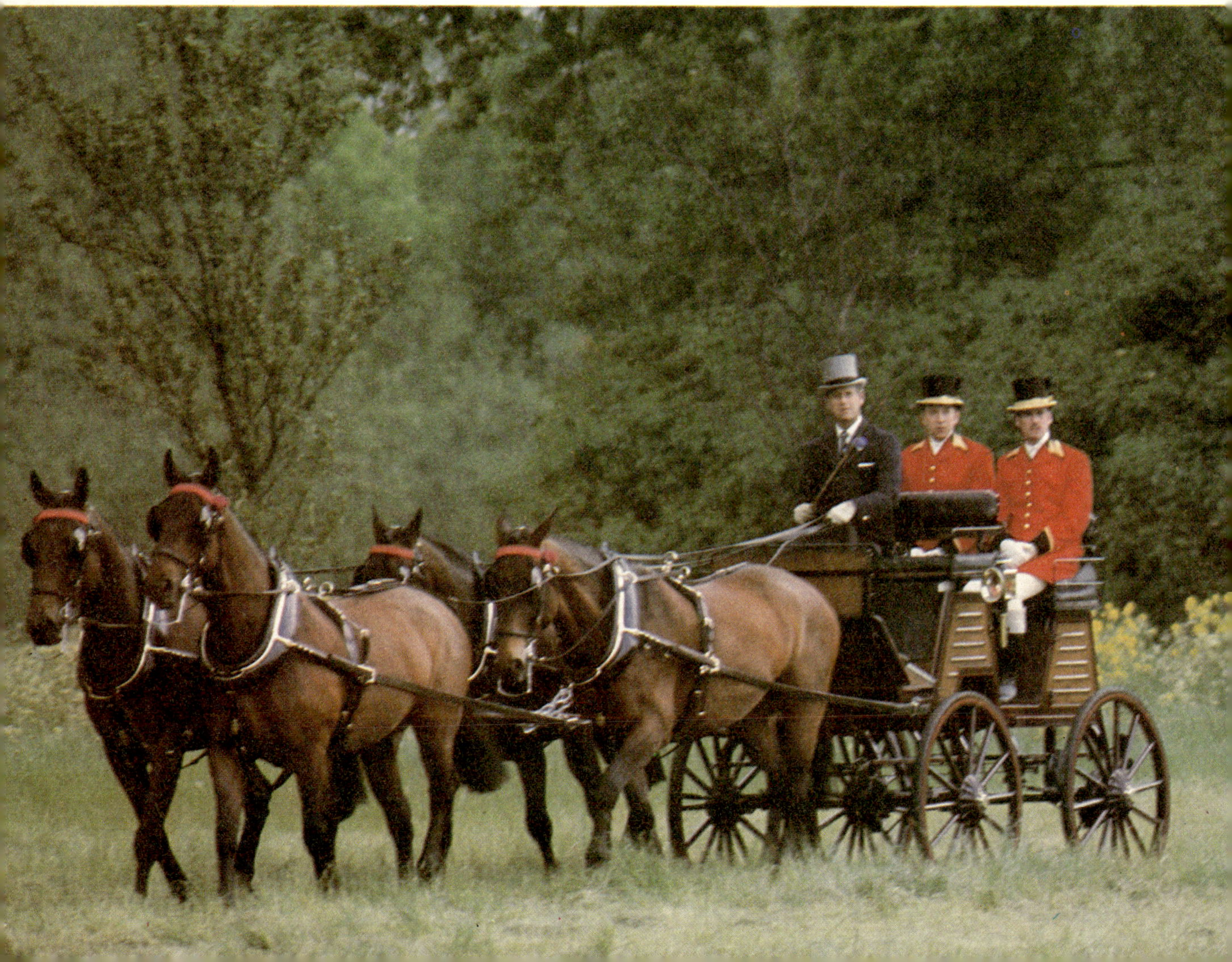

The following spring the Duke of Edinburgh was competing himself. One of his first outings was to the two-day carriage driving trials at Lowther Castle near Penrith in Westmorland. The Duke, driving a Balmoral dog cart drawn by four thoroughbred Cleveland Bays, finished seventh. Sir John won the event.

At the Royal Windsor Horse Show the Duke was unlucky. He had to retire from the marathon when the back axle of the dog cart was badly bent as he negotiated a narrow bridge.

But for a beginner he did well later in the year, being placed fourth at the Lowther trials and second in the obstacle driving section of the European championships.

1974 began badly for the Duke. He was bruised and badly shaken when a wagonette and four he was driving in the grounds of Windsor Castle overturned and he was kicked by one of the

In the collecting ring the Duke prepares for competition

Top left: A tense moment for the Duke at the water during the World Championships at Windsor in 1980

Far left: Decked out for the Dressage, the royal bays make a splendid sight

Overleaf top right: Prince Charles has a go at trotting in Fife in 1978

Overleaf bottom right: Colonel Sir John Miller, the Crown Equerry, who taught Prince Philip to drive

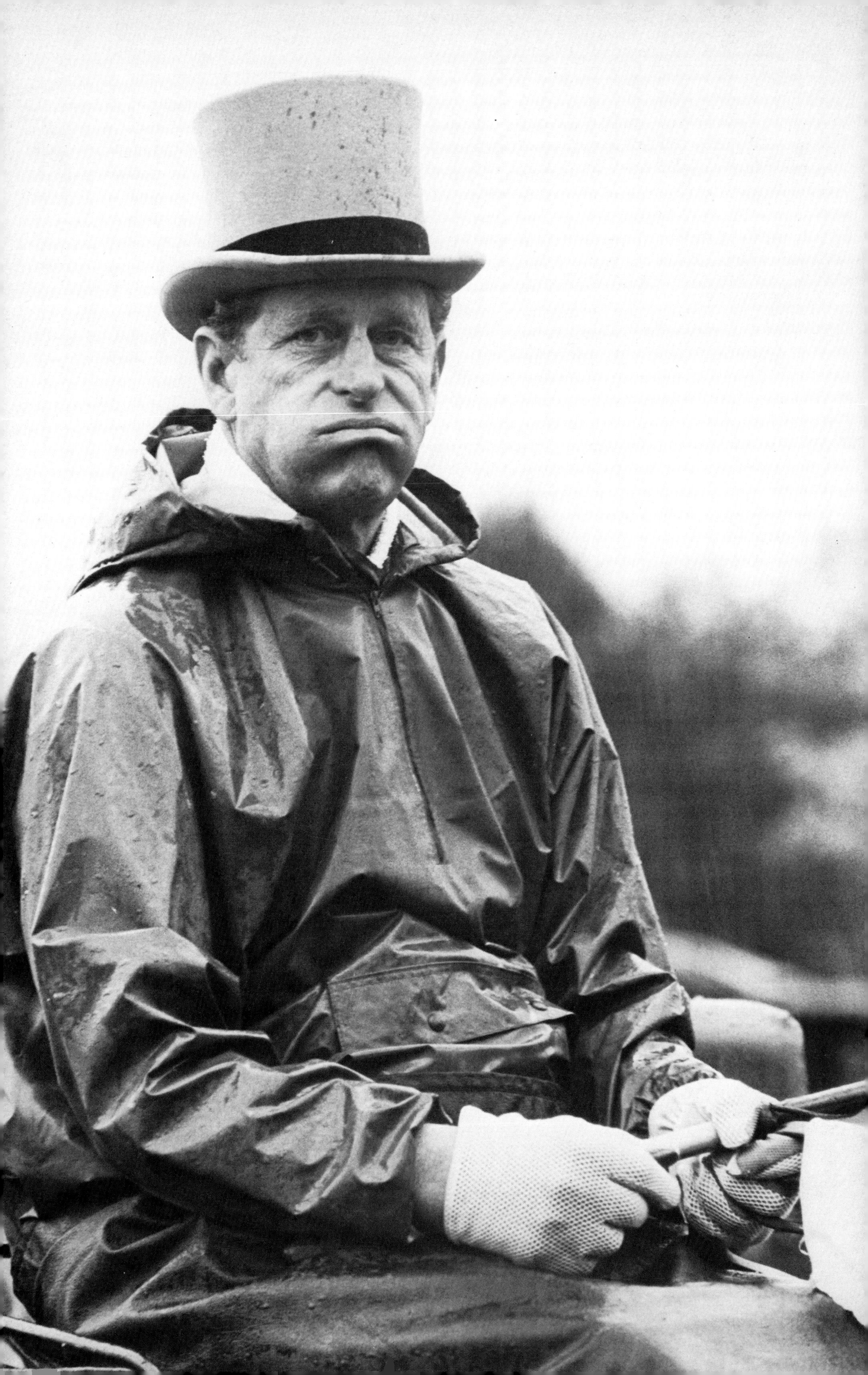

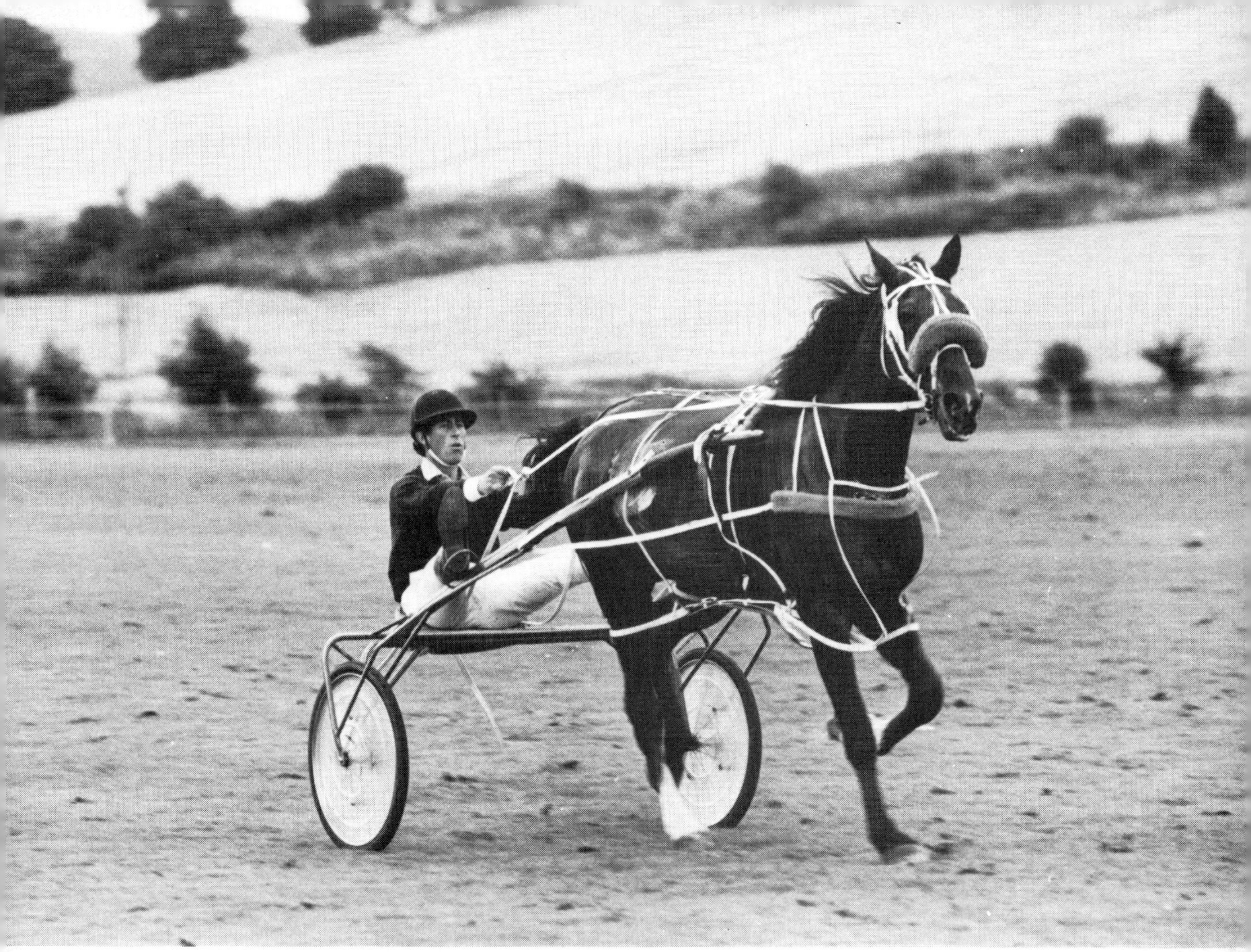

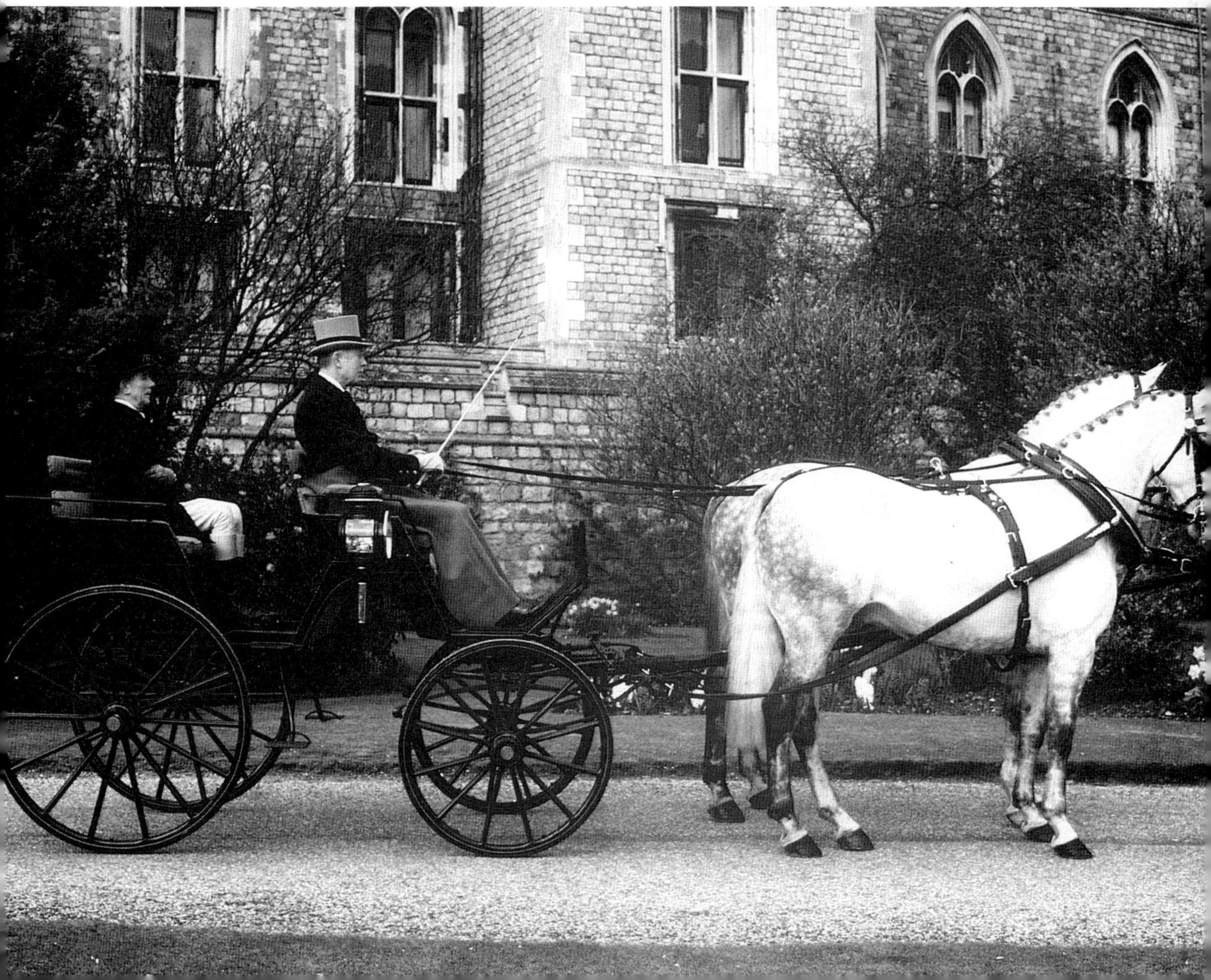

Princess Anne and Prince Edward in a pony cart

Opposite: Prince Philip nattily dressed for driving

horses; and at the Lowther trials he had to jump to safety when his lightweight open carriage toppled over when one of the four horses drawing it stumbled on a tree stump. The Duke sportingly took the blame. "I had two absolutely literally green horses. It was very stupid. They were not up to it and I don't think it was very sensible," he said.

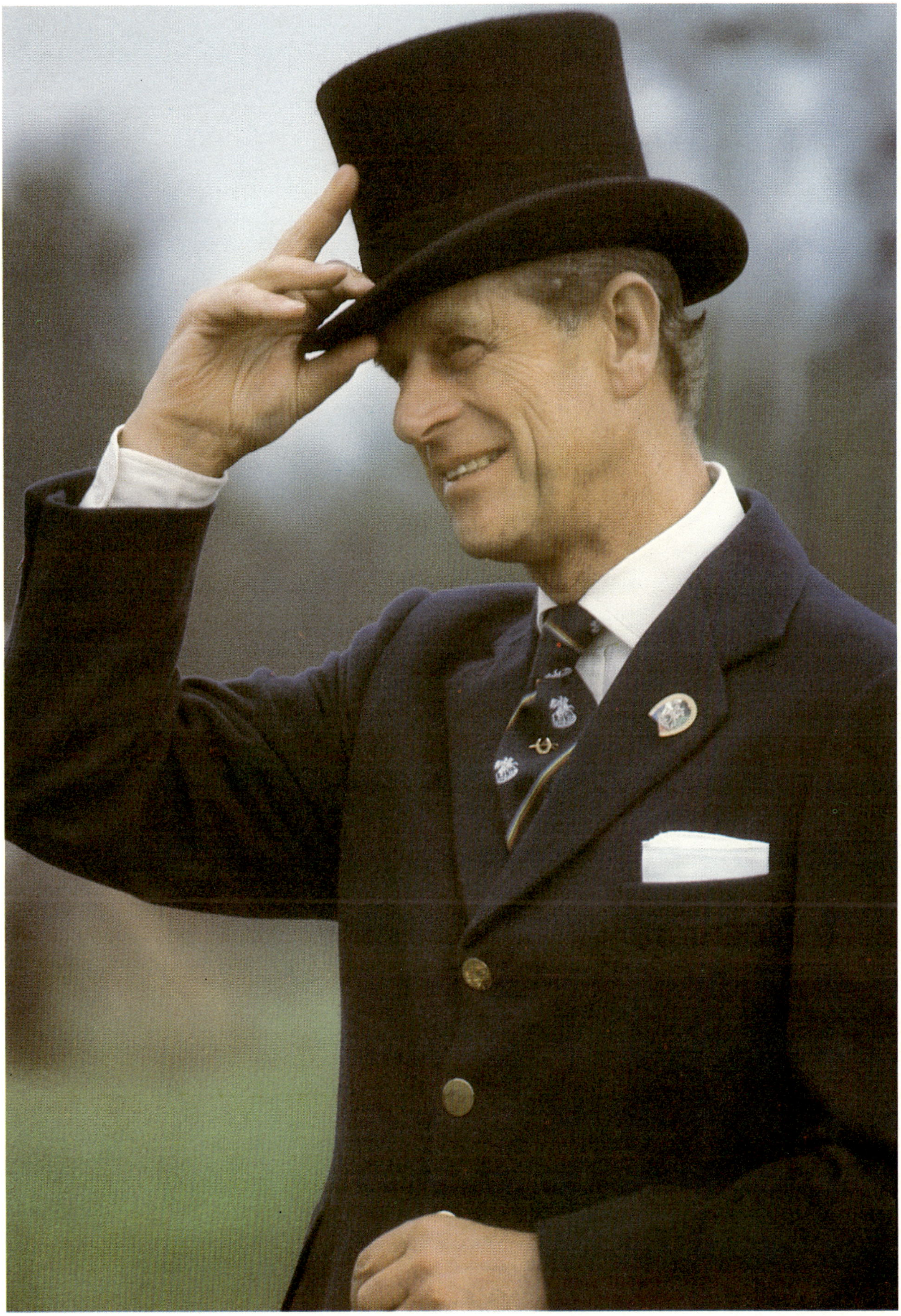

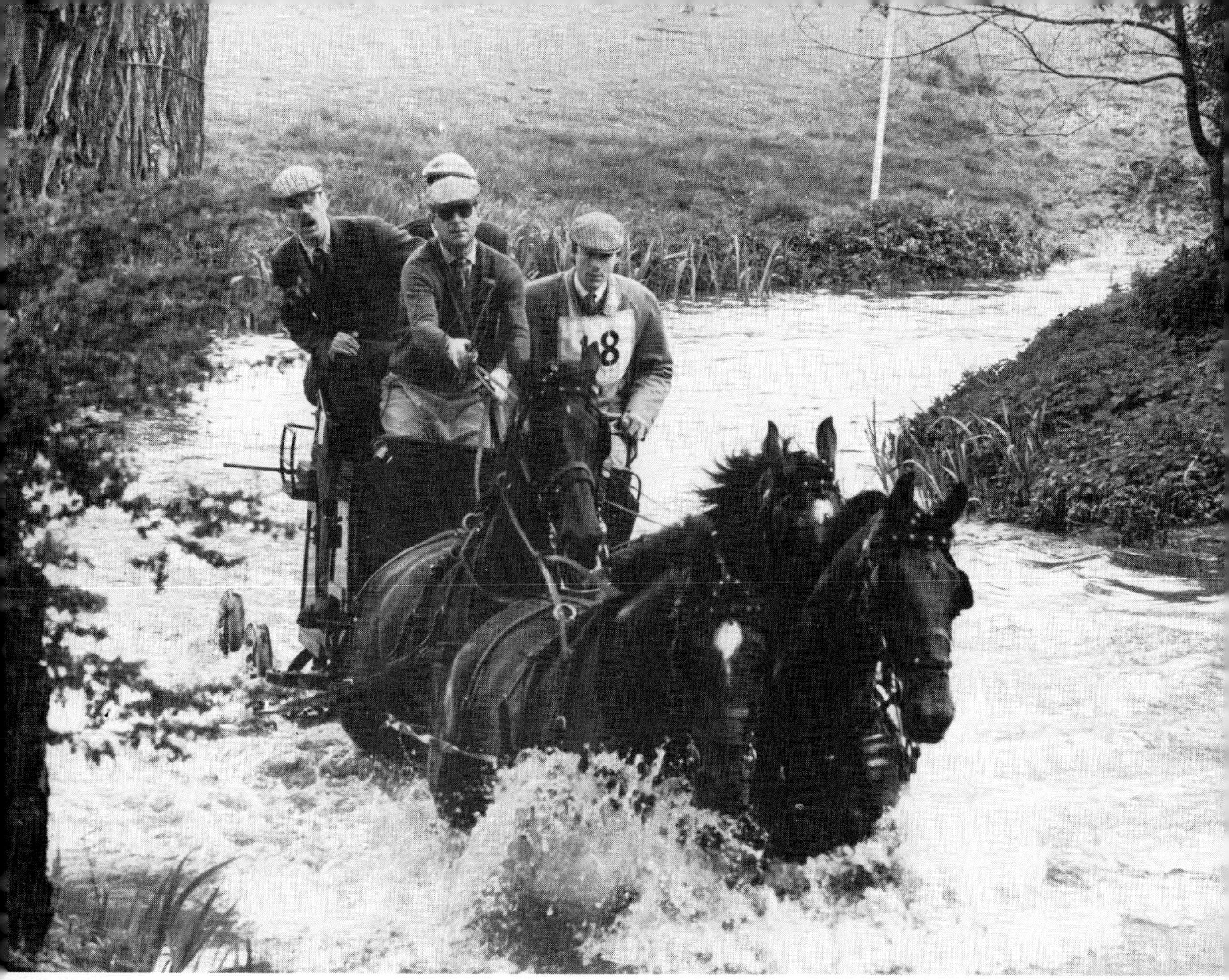

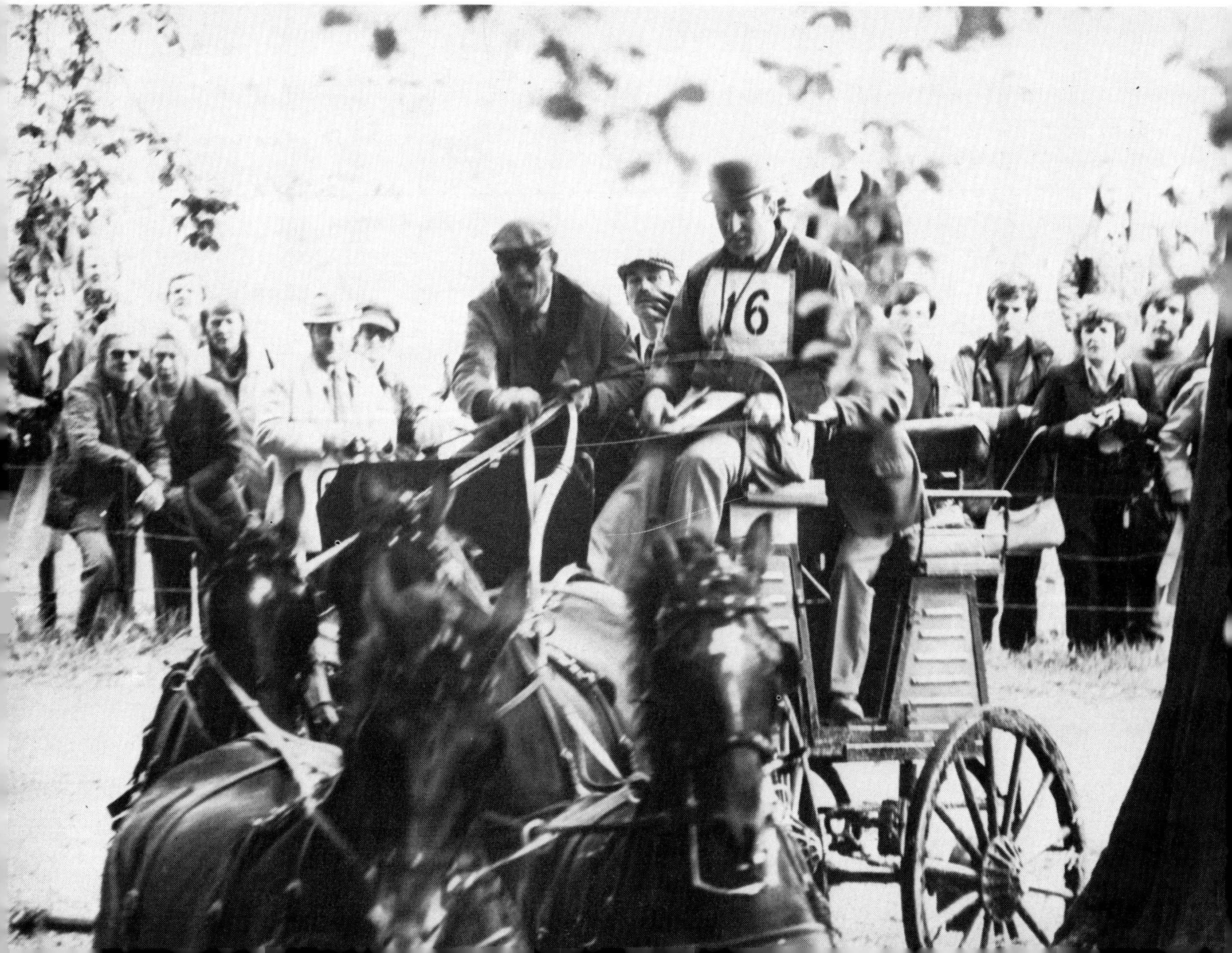

The driver's apron is designed for elegance and warmth

Although he continued to drive successfully, the Duke failed to make the British team for World Carriage Driving that year, but in 1975 he was picked for the team for the International Driving Trials in Poland. "It is the first time I have represented Britain at anything. I am very much the tailend Charlie in this team. All I hope to do is to get round and I might finish about twentieth on form," he said modestly. In fact he completed the course and came eighteenth.

Despite a mishap when his dog cart and pair bolted at Smith's Lawn narrowly missing parked cars, the Duke of Edinburgh went on to compete at the 1976 World Championships in the

Top left: Another fine picture of the Queen's team at full tilt

Far left: The Duke urges his team to greater efforts

71

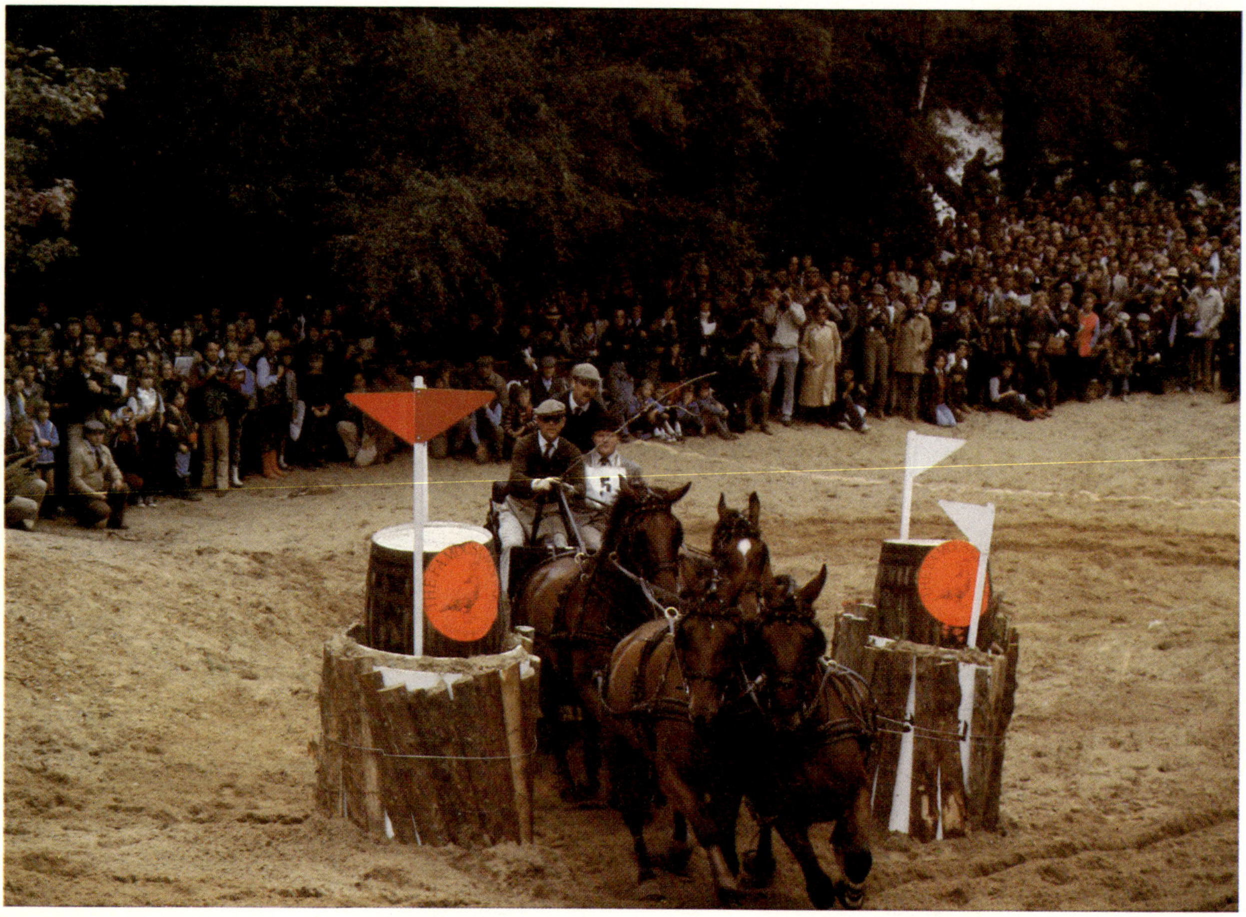

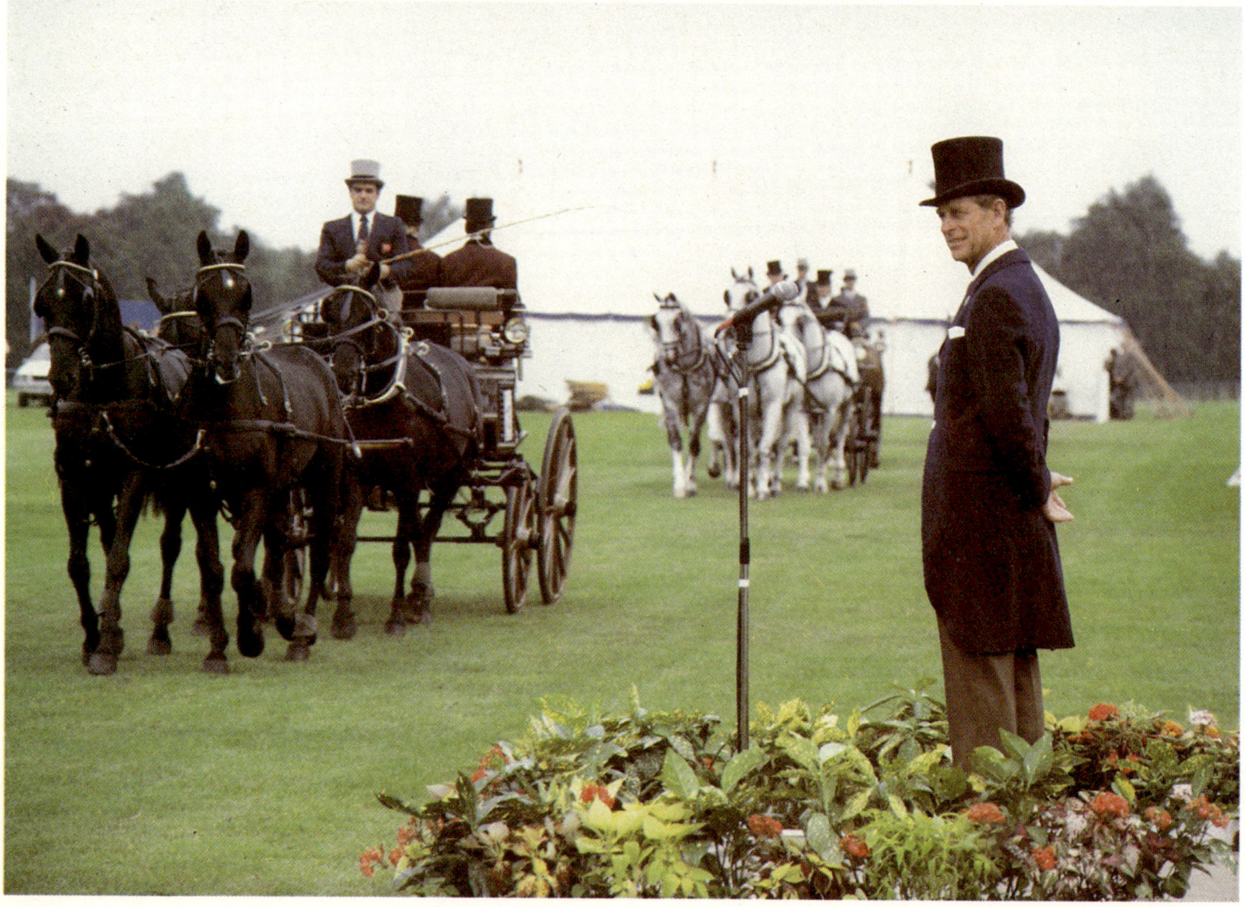

Netherlands. He gamely completed the course after three of the bars to which the leader's traces were attached had broken.

Later that year he was awarded the Martini International Club's driving medallion in recognition of the notable part he had played in establishing driving as part of the equestrian sports scene.

In 1977 the Duke of Edinburgh was runner up in the Barclays Bank International Grand Prix driving a team of the Queen's bays. He came second in the cross-country marathon and the

Windsor Castle makes a spectacular background as the carriages drive along the Long Walk

Top left: In the sandpit at Windsor during the 1980 World Championships

Far left: The Duke, as President of the Driving Association, takes the salute

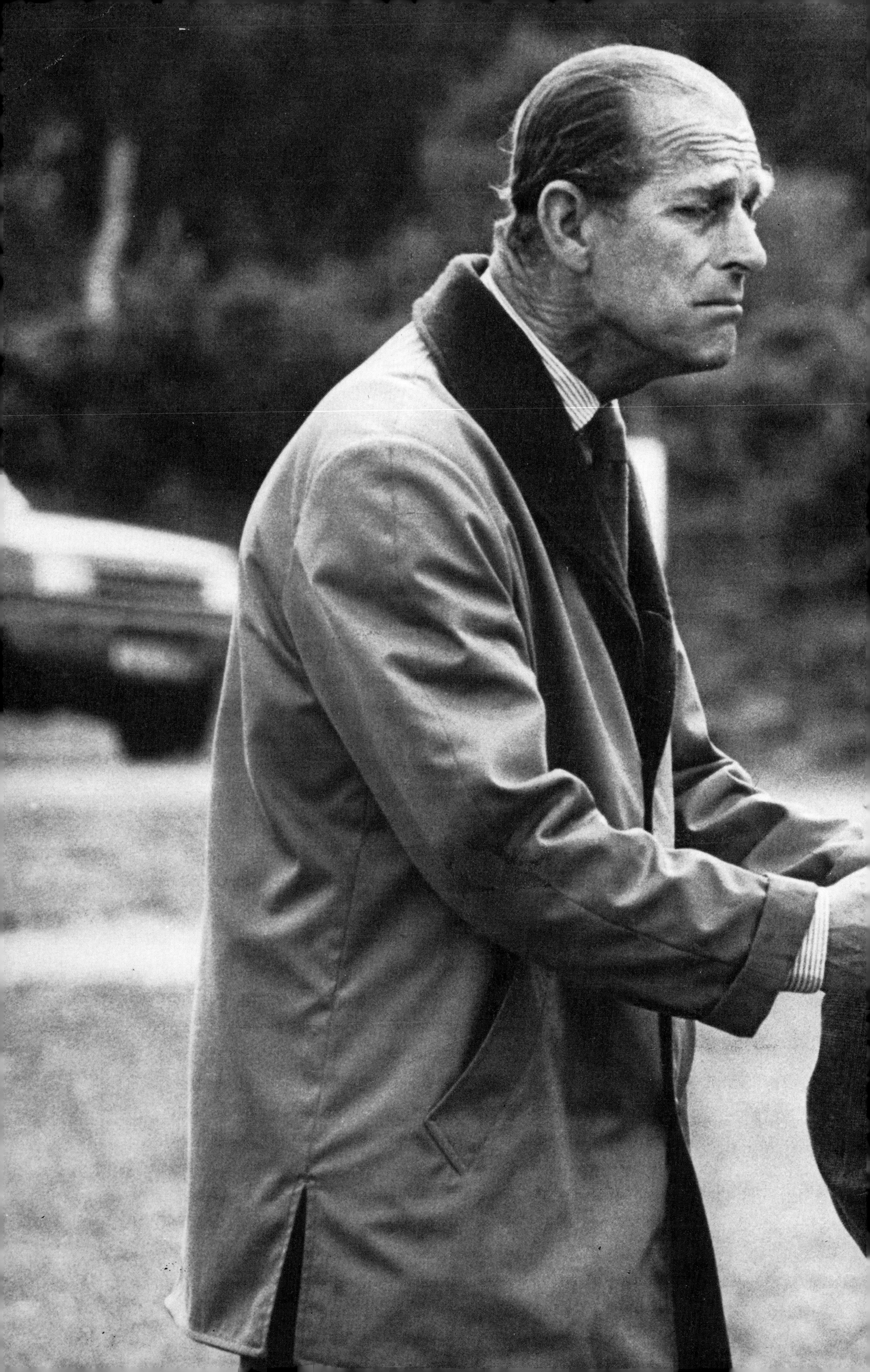

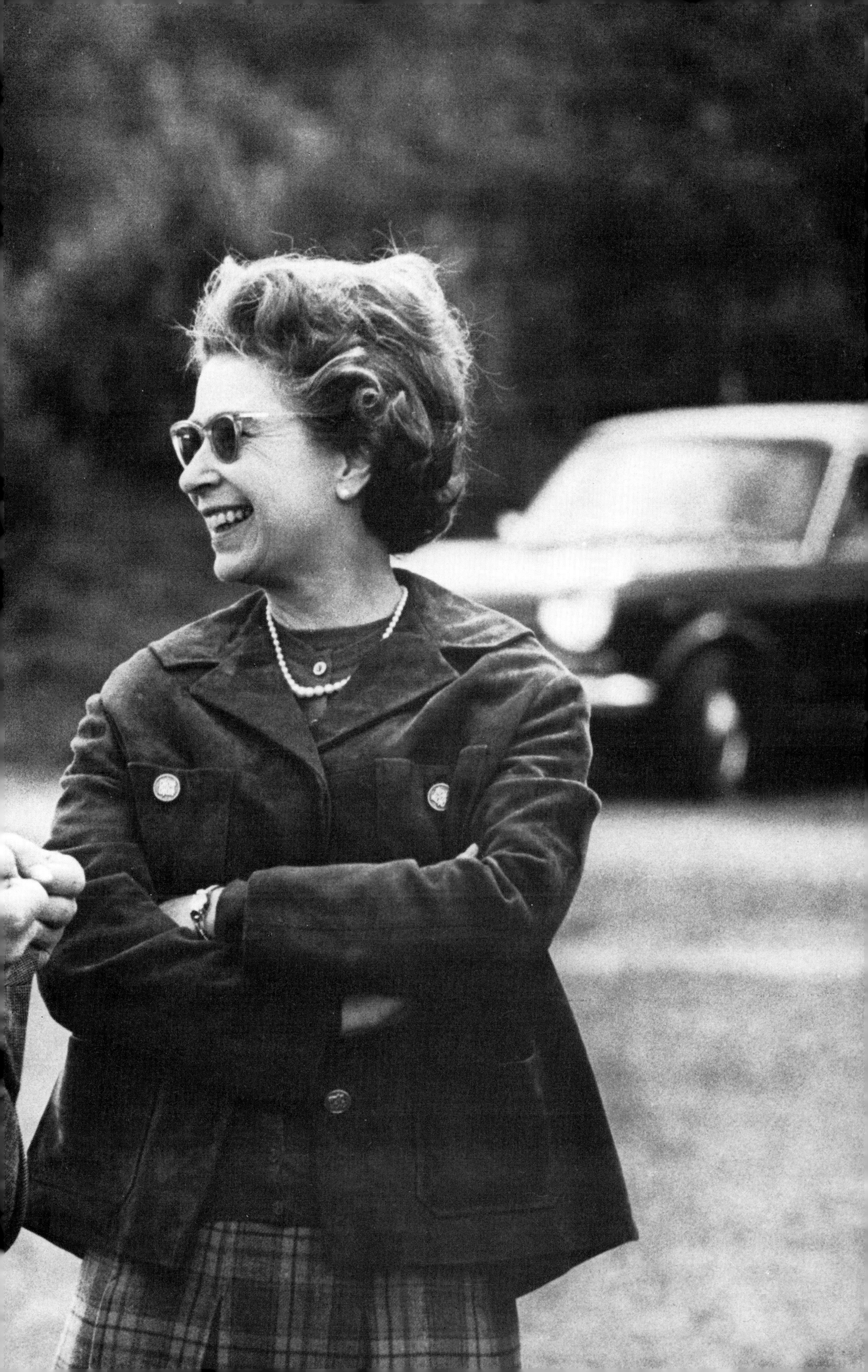

Prince Andrew draws the Queen's attention towards the action

Previous page: Every picture tells a story

obstacle events at the National Driving Championships at Goodwood and won his class in the presentation and dressage.

The following year he competed in the World Driving Championships in Hungary for the British team which finished third. The coach he was driving overturned when one wheel hit a shepherd's hut but the carriage was righted and he finished the race.

He came second in the Grand Prix at the Royal Windsor Horse Show in 1979, but an accident on the gruelling marathon course at the Lowther Trials cost him his lead.

Bad luck also dogged him in the National Championships when a wheel caught in a post, a trace snapped and the horses bolted. He finished sixth.

In 1980 the Duke led the British challenge in the World Championships which were held at Windsor. His team won the gold medal.

Prince Philip in the royal dog cart

In 1981 he won the final obstacle stage and finished second overall in the Grand Prix at the Royal Windsor Horse Show with a team of the Queen's Cleveland bays and Oldenburger crossbreds. He was third in the championships held at Scone Palace and won the three-day competition at the Royal Norfolk Agricultural Show at Costessey. In August the British team led by the Duke won the bronze medal in the European Championships at Zug in Switzerland.

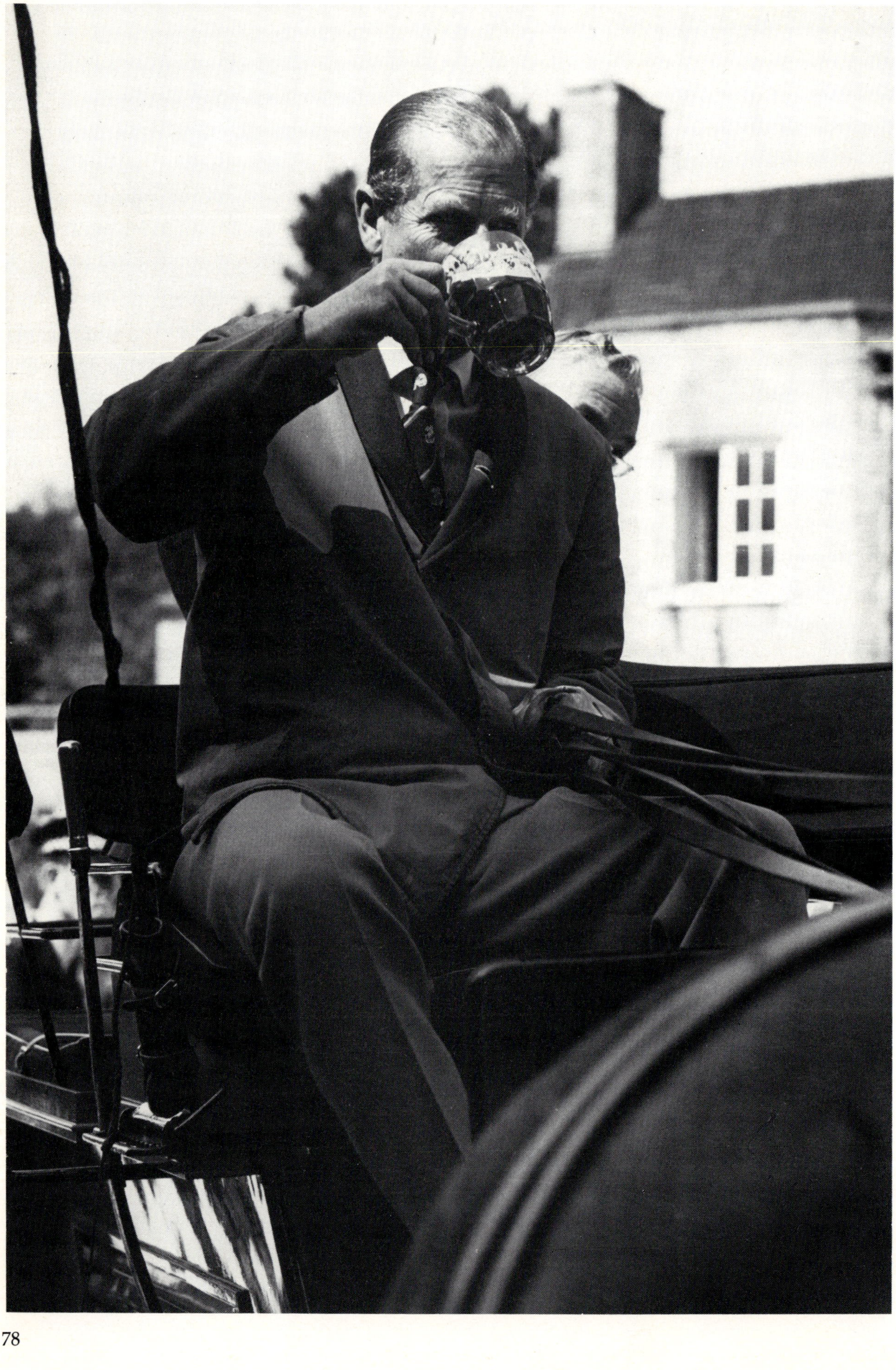

Princess Anne at the water at Osberton Horse Trials

EVENTING AND SHOWJUMPING

PRINCESS ANNE admits that she has no other real interests apart from eventing and showjumping. "If you're really involved with horses and want to be successful with them – you know, not just play at it – they don't leave you much time for anything else. You have to look after them," she said in a recent interview.

Such dedication won the Princess the European Championship at twenty-one and made her the first member of the royal family to do so. Her husband Captain Mark Phillips is also a seasoned and successful competitor. He won the World Championship in 1970, the European Championship in 1971, and helped Britain win a gold medal at the 1972 Olympic Games at Munich.

Opposite: Driving is thirsty work

The Princess gets herself out of trouble during the cross country section of the Amberley Horse Trials

Horses brought the Princess and Captain Phillips together and both learned to ride young. The Princess inherited her mother's love of riding and was in the saddle by the time she was four. Her interest was nurtured during her years at Benenden, her public school, and soon after leaving she took part in the Horse of the Year Show at Wembley. Captain Phillips says he cannot remember when he first started riding but like the Princess, he was a keen and active member of the Pony Club, attending many rallies.

He does admit that the first time he was selected for a club team his horse refused three times at the water jump. At Marlborough, Captain Phillips 'lived for sport' and took part in rugger and athletics. His speciality was the long jump and he represented Wiltshire. "But when I had to choose, riding won. I longed to ride in adult horse trials and have the Union Jack on my saddle," he said.

Preparing for Dressage

Opposite: Captain Mark Phillips is not only a keen competitor but also a skilled trainer

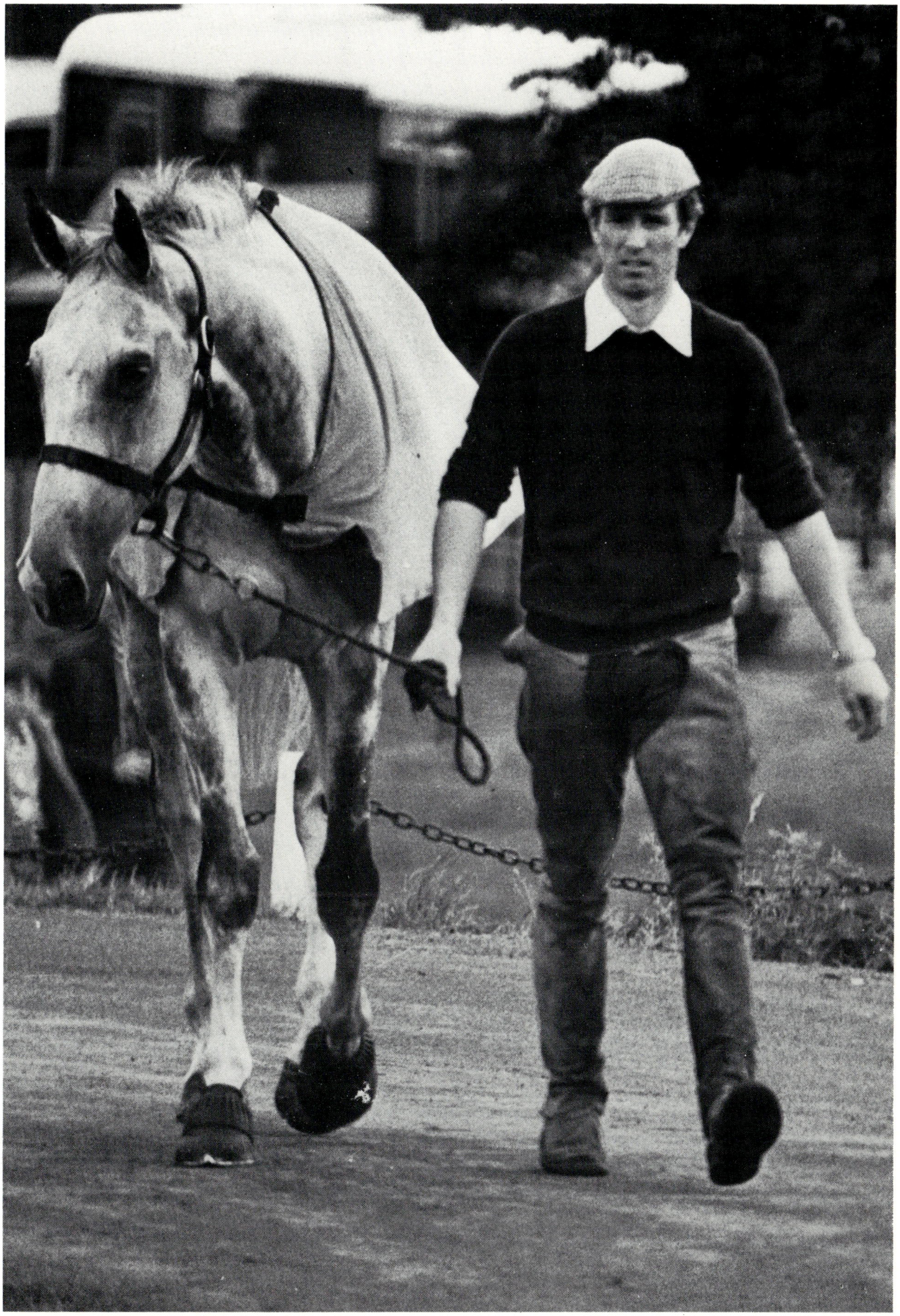

A fine shot of Princess Anne during the cross country at Tidworth

A relaxed moment for Princess Anne and Mark Phillips at Amberley

Opposite: Mark Phillips with Princess Alexandra and the Hon Angus Ogilvy

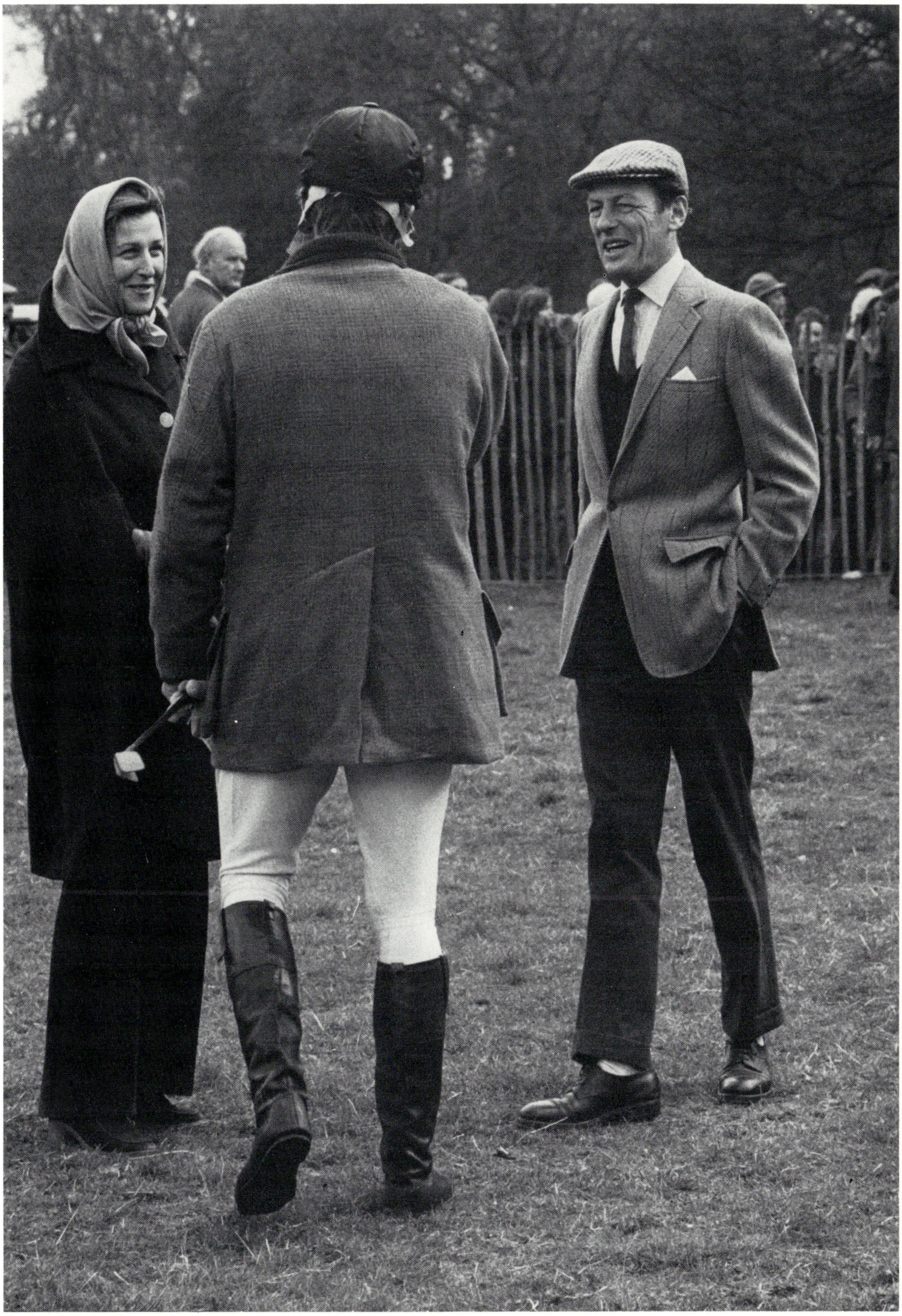

Captain Mark Phillips competing in the show jumping section

Opposite: Mark Phillips with his son Peter at Burghley

Captain Phillips' first real chance came when he was eighteen and had just entered the Royal Military Academy at Sandhurst. Colonel Bill Lithgow, then manager of the British eventing team and commander of Captain Phillips' college, found a way for him to compete at the Burghley Horse Trials. Captain Phillips finished fourth – a dramatically good result for a newcomer. Six months later he again came fourth in the most important of all three-day events, Badminton, and later in 1968 was chosen as Britain's reserve rider for the Mexico Olympics. He did not actually get a chance to ride but as he says: "It all went on from there."

Meanwhile the Princess was competing in numerous horse trials and in 1971 reached international level on her home-bred horse Doublet, winning the European three-day event.

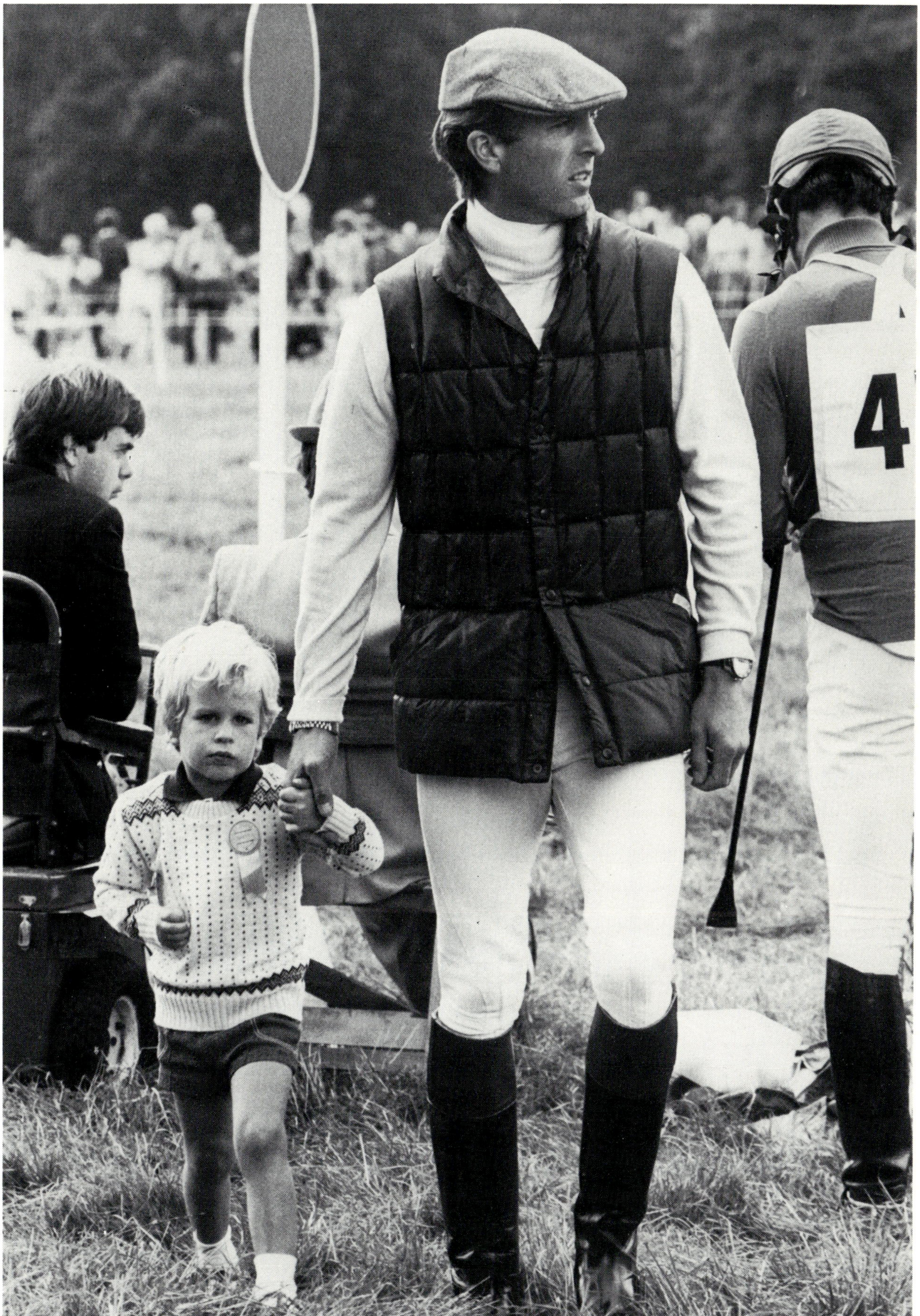
4

The British team for the Montreal Olympics. From left, Lucinda Prior-Palmer, Princess Anne, Richard Meade, Hugh Thomas and Mark Phillips

1971 was a glorious year for Princess Anne. She was named sportswoman of the year three times, first by the Sports Writers' Association, then by the Daily Express and finally by World Sport, the journal of the British Olympic Association. She also became BBC television's Sports Personality of the year.

She lost her European title in Kiev, in Russia in 1973 but two years later she was picked for the British team to compete in Germany and won silver medals both as an individual and as a team member.

Prince Charles competing in a show jumping competition at Ascot in aid of Stoke Mandeville Hospital

Opposite: Princess Anne beneath the equestrian statue of Prince Albert at Smith's Lawn

86

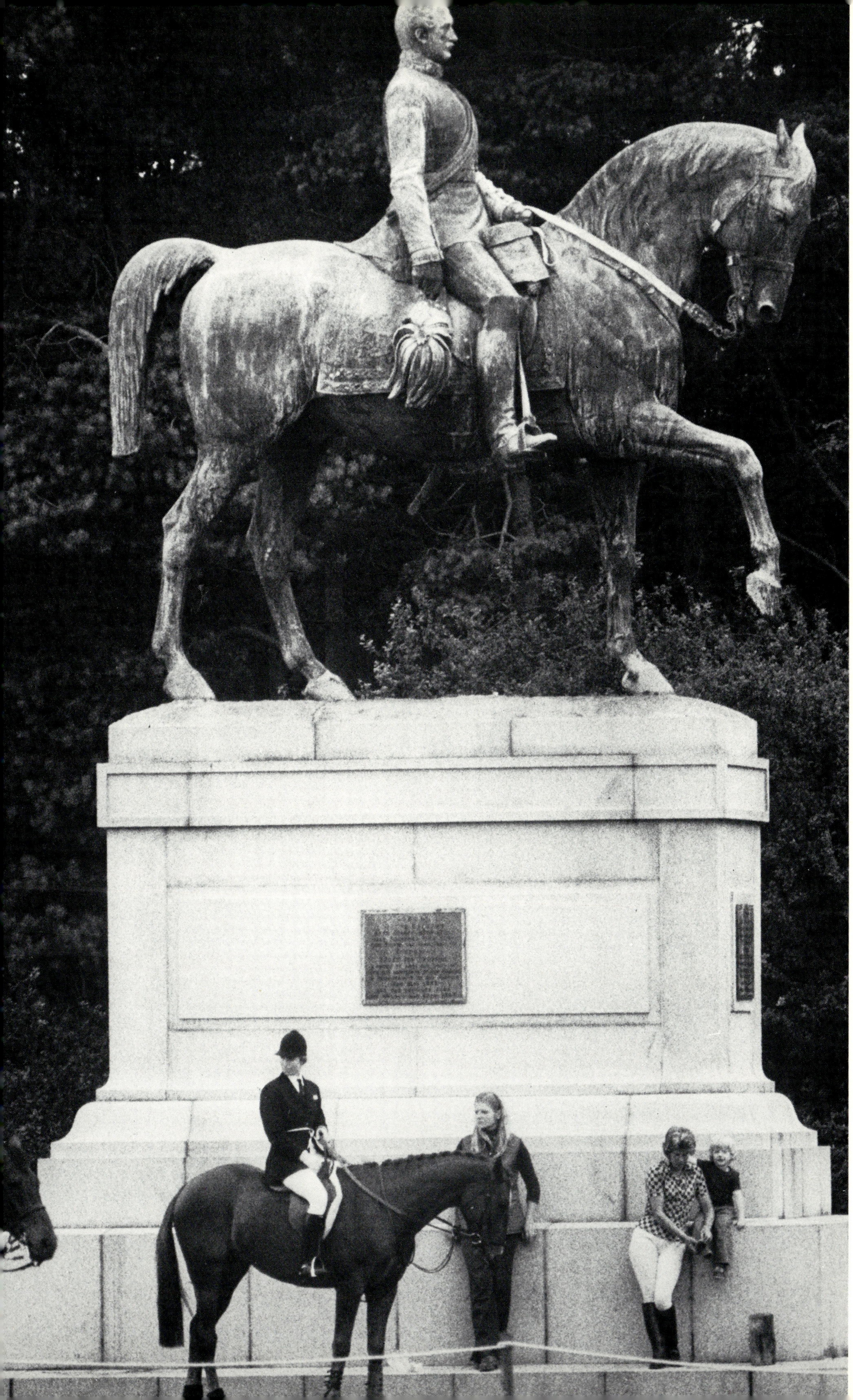

Prince Charles and Prince Edward riding amongst the crowds at Badminton

Her one remaining ambition, to ride for Britain in the Olympics, was fulfilled the following year when she competed in Montreal as a member of the three-day event team.

Meanwhile Captain Phillips was having successes of his own. He is one of only two people to have won the three-day event at Badminton four times and he did so in 1971, 1972, 1974 and 1981. He was unlucky not to win the 1974 World Championship on the Queen's horse Columbus. He was leading when the horse went lame after the cross-country.

The birth of the Princess's son Peter in the Queen's Silver Jubilee year put an end to her riding activities for some time but she was back in the saddle at Sandringham within three months.

In 1979 the royal couple again did well at Badminton. Captain Phillips finished third and the Princess sixth. But they had to pull out of the European three day event after the Princess's horse Goodwill was retired and her husband's mount Columbus went lame.

An equestrian star of the future; Peter Phillips riding Smokey, his Shetland pony

Later that year they caused some controversy when Captain Phillips accepted a three year sponsorship worth £60,000 from British Leyland. However he explained his decision. "Princess Anne is as aware of our financial position as I am and we decided we would have to cut back or find money from sponsorship. We are a young couple with a mortgage and we had to think hard about it all. It costs at least £3,000 a year to keep one horse in training."

Princess Anne at the Wylie Horse Trials

The Queen, with Prince Philip watching, presents the Whitbread Trophy to Mark Phillips on his fourth victory in the Badminton Horse Trials

Because Britain's equestrian team pulled out of the Moscow Olympics last year neither of the royal pair had a chance to compete. Captain Phillips was thought to have been likely to have won a place in the British team but the Princess did not have a horse of sufficient calibre. The birth of her daughter Zara kept Princess Anne out of the saddle for some months.

But in September she made her first appearance since the birth, competing at Burghley at a three-day horse trial. Unfortunately her horse, the Queen's Stevie B, lost its footing at the water jump and the Princess was thrown from the saddle. Captain Phillips also fell at the water.

Already though a new generation of royal eventers is on the way. Peter Phillips received a ten-year old Palomino gelding called Trigger on his fourth birthday.

George V at the wheel of the cutter Britannia in 1924

MAKING A SPLASH

THE BRITISH royal family have a long naval tradition and the present generation is no exception. Both the Duke of Edinburgh and Prince Charles have served in the Royal Navy and Prince Andrew is currently undergoing naval training.

It therefore comes as no surprise that they enjoy many sports connected with water including windsurfing, sailing, sub-aqua diving and water-skiing.

Prince Charles, whether through natural sporting talent or dogged determination, seems to manage to keep abreast of the rest of the royal family. He is expert in many water sports and always keen to try new ones.

The royal children had the advantage of a private pool at Buckingham Palace and, with the active encouragement of their parents, learned to swim young. But the Princess of Wales is the only member of the royal family to have won cups for the sport. She won no less than four while at her public school, West Heath, near Sevenoaks in Kent.

Prince Charles surfaces after diving to the Mary Rose

Opposite: The Prince preparing to dive beneath the Arctic ice cap at Resolute Bay

Prince Charles first became interested in sub-aqua diving during his service years when undergoing helicopter training. It was then necessary to learn the proper procedure for escaping from a ditched aircraft and he soon became expert in underwater swimming.

While in Canada he tested his skills to the full by diving under the Arctic ice cap. More recently he had made exploratory excursions down to the wreck of the Tudor warship the *Mary Rose*.

The Queen enjoys swimming, although of a less adventurous kind, and frequently takes a dip when the royal yacht *Britannia* is cruising through the warmer oceans of the world. Her idea of a perfect day off during a royal tour is a barbecue picnic on the beach of a nearby island, a brisk walk and a swim if possible.

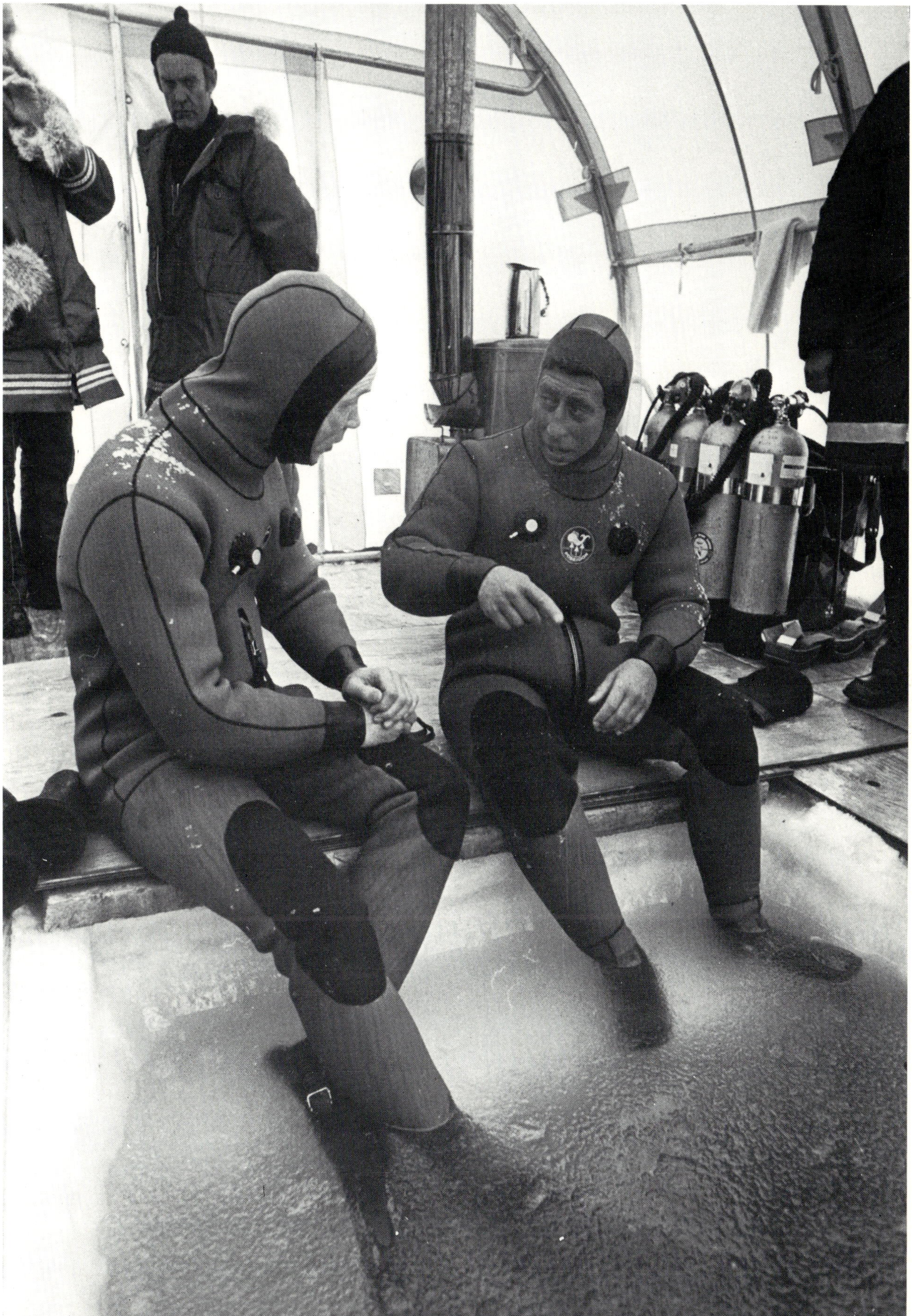

Prince Andrew at the wheel of a speedboat at Cowes

Prince Charles waterskiing in Fiji

Opposite: Prince Edward windsurfing at Cowes

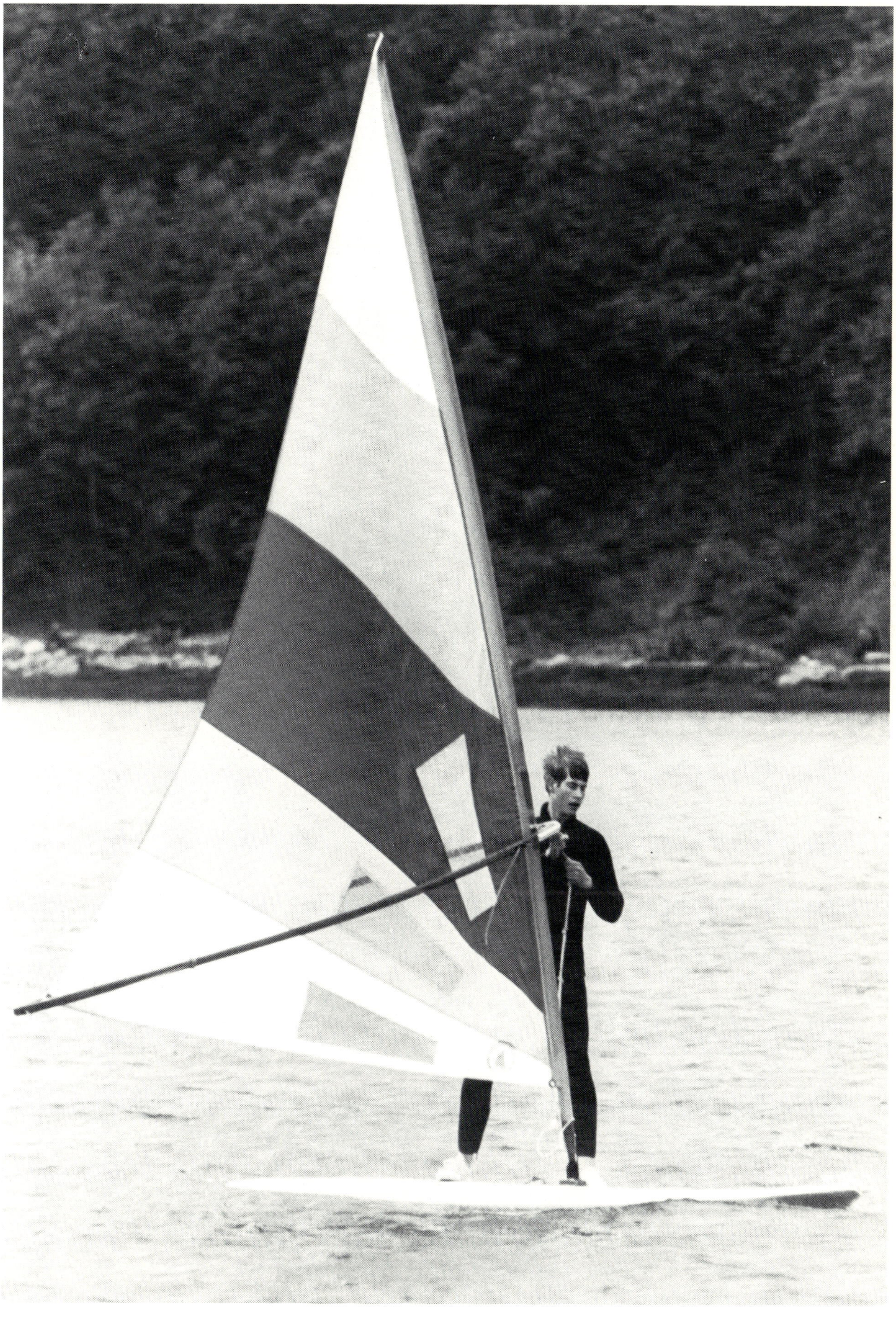

The Duke of Edinburgh and Uffa Fox preparing for a day's sailing in Coweslip in 1953

Opposite top: Prince Charles jogging on the beach at Perth in Western Austrialia

Far right: The Prince swimming in the surf

However, on one occasion the royal party got more then they bargained for. During the Queen's Caribbean tour in her Jubilee Year, they were spending a lazy day swimming and picnicking when one of the police officers assigned to the tour who was keen on sub-aqua diving, discovered a shark basking behind a nearby coral reef. A hasty exit from the water followed, although the officer assured them that the shark was harmless and invited them to come and look.

Prince Charles and Prince Edward go windsurfing with varying degrees of success. Prince Charles was one of the first to obtain a windsurfer and wisely learnt to master its precarious skills in the comparative privacy of a flooded gravel pit near Windsor before trying his luck in public during Cowes Week. He is now very proficient at the sport and his youngest brother, although forced to take an unexpected swim quite frequently, is also improving fast.

97

Princess Margaret and friends going waterskiing in Mustique

Both Prince Charles and Princess Margaret water-ski, though rarely in public. Prince Andrew took up canoeing during his time at his Canadian school, Lakefield College. But the favourite royal water sport must be sailing. The royal yacht *Britannia* has become as much a part of Cowes Week in the Isle of Wight as the Royal Yacht Squadron or the endless social round of cocktail parties and balls. Only a royal honeymoon kept *Britannia* away last year and even then a humbler substitute – in the shape of the Trinity House supply ship *Patricia* – was found.

The Duke of Edinburgh never misses Cowes even if other commitments mean that he cannot stay as long as he would like. He is a keen competitor. His great sailing friend was Uffa Fox – famed almost equally for his seamanship and his rendering of sea shanties. They met shortly after the Second World War when the Duke was looking for a teacher 'with a bit of commonsense'. It was the beginning of a lifelong friendship. Rarely were the two men apart during Cowes Week and when Uffa Fox died aged seventy-four in 1972 it was the end of a sailing era for the Duke.

The Duke said of him later: "He was the best crewman you could wish for. At sea occasions arise when you have to bark. Uffa was very good at that."

Even with the best partnerships mistakes do happen. Once when the pair were racing in the Dragon class yacht *Bluebottle* – given to the Queen and the Duke of Edinburgh as a wedding

Prince Andrew in his Flying Fifteen at Cowes

Princess Anne and Prince Philip aboard Yeoman XVI

Prince Charles at the helm of the Australian yacht Siska

present by the Island Sailing Club – they sped into the lead only to find after a few minutes that they were going the wrong way. As soon as the error was discovered, (after about a quarter of a mile) *Bluebottle*, with the Duke at the helm and Mr Fox crewing, turned round and set off in hot pursuit of the other fourteen yachts. They managed to finish sixth.

Mr Fox commented: "The Duke is a marvellous helmsman to the windward. He is quicker than anybody else to react to the least change in the wind. It should be remembered that the Duke is only able to race once a year in *Bluebottle*. If he could race as often as some of the people down here he would be the finest helmsman in the country."

In 1962 *Bluebottle*, in which Britain had won a bronze medal in the 1956 Melbourne Olympics, was withdrawn from racing and put at the disposal of the Royal Naval College, Dartmouth. The royal family hoped this would encourage all types of yachting.

To replace her came an even more famous boat, the 34-ton yawl *Bloodhound* – the winner of the Fastnet ocean race, the Cowes-Dinard race, the round the Isle of Wight race and twice winner of the Cowes-Plymouth event. The purchase price was said to be £10,000 and when she was sold nearly twenty years later, she went for £65,000.

The Duke at the helm of Yeoman XVI

It was on *Bloodhound* that Prince Charles and Princess Anne learned to sail. The Duke of Edinburgh took the yacht from Land's End to the Firth of Clyde for a family sailing holiday in 1962 and it was such a success that he did the same again the following year. In her first full sailing season *Bloodhound* went 6,700 nautical miles and in 1965, with the Duke at the helm, she finished fourth in the New York Yacht Club Challenge Cup – although she was placed twelfth on handicap. The Queen, busy with her younger children Prince Andrew and Prince Edward, rarely went out on *Bloodhound* and in recent years has not been to Cowes. Princess Alexandra with her husband the Hon Angus Ogilvy and their children James and Marina, is nearly always on board *Britannia*. She is a good helmswoman and with Prince Charles and Princess Anne went out to meet Chay Blyth when he returned to port from his round the world voyage in 1971.

Another royal yacht was the Flying Fifteen *Coweslip*. She was sailed with some success not only by the Duke and Mr Fox but also by the younger members of the royal family. However, in recent years the Duke of Edinburgh has tended to sail in Owen Aisher's *Yeoman* yachts while Prince Andrew and Prince Edward have raced in John Terry's Flying Fifteen, *Spanish Lady*. Prince Charles does still go out, as he did with King Constantine of

Prince Edward and Lady Sarah Spencer at Cowes

Greece, but now often prefers to windsurf instead. But he may go back to boats. The Princess of Wales likes sailing and was seen out on the water with Prince Edward two years ago.

In a small boat members of the royal family can for once escape the attention of the faithful police bodyguard, who otherwise accompany them everywhere. Britain may no longer rule the waves, but Britain's royal family still enjoy spending as much time on them as possible.

Prince Michael of Kent with his brakeman Michael Sweet competing in the 1971 World Bobsleigh Championships in Cervinia

WINTER SPORTS

THE FIRST time the royal children experienced the cold hard realities of winter sports was in their early teens. Both Prince Charles and Princess Anne were sent off to Richmond Ice rink in 1962 to learn how to skate. They could not have found a better teacher than Mrs Betty Calloway, a former National Skating Association gold medallist, who had already taught film stars James Mason and Claire Bloom how to skate. In those pre-inflation days the royal youngsters were charged eight shillings for a twenty minute lesson and Prince Charles was so keen that he had four lessons in as many days. Perhaps for his own protection as much as that of other skaters, the beginner Prince was given the small figure skating rink to himself for practice but despite such early promise he doesn't seem to have continued with the sport.

Prince Andrew, who in his turn went to Richmond five years later, was more enthusiastic. Within hours of arriving at his Canadian school, Lakefield College in Ontario in 1978 he was lured out onto the ice for a game of hockey and promptly scored two goals.

Prince Charles with a motorised sledge in the Arctic

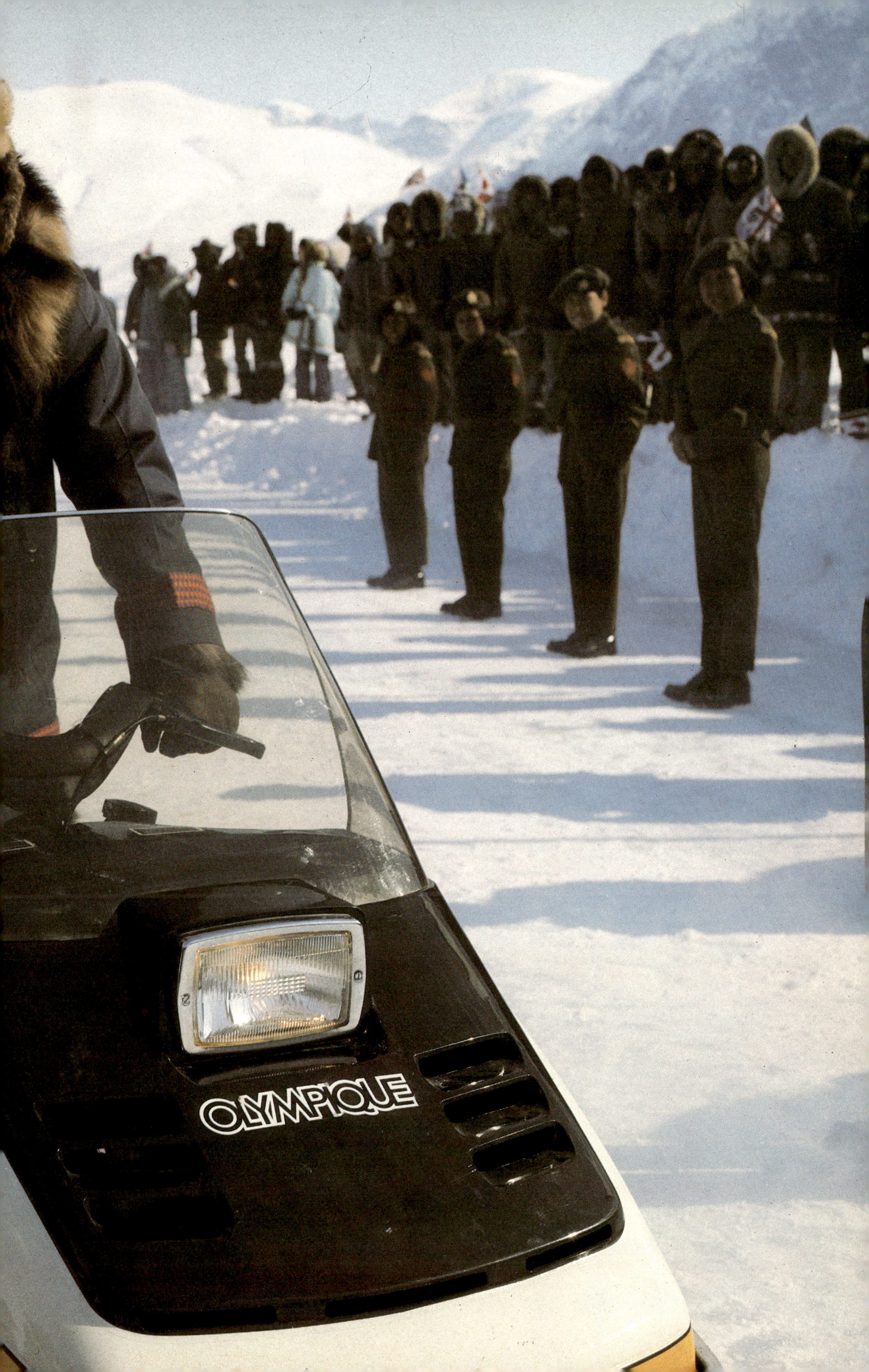
OLYMPIQUE

The Duke of Kent at St Moritz, skiing for his regiment the Royal Scots Greys

Top right: The Duchess on holiday at the same time

Skiing must be the favourite royal winter sport. The Duke and Duchess of Gloucester have been going skiing for many years and all four of the Queen's children enjoy the sport although Princess Anne sometimes prefers tobogganing as does Prince Michael of Kent though of a rather advanced kind. A veteran of the famed and dangerous Cresta Run, Prince Michael is President of the British Bobsleigh team. Even the royal family's latest member, the Princess of Wales, is keen on winter sports. She spent several months at a Swiss finishing school at Videmanette near Gstaad as a sixteen-year-old after leaving school and became an accomplished skier.

Prince Charles was fourteen when he went on his first skiing holiday and invested in a pair of blue skis before he had even inspected the slopes, so confident was he that he would like the sport. Prince Charles went on holiday with the Duke of Edinburgh's sister Princess Sophia and her husband Prince Georg of Hanover at the spa resort of Tarasp in Switzerland. The village in the lower Engadine is in the same valley as the better known St Moritz, has a few hundred inhabitants and is watched over by a magnificent mediaeval castle. The castle belongs to one of Prince Philip's many European cousins, Prince Ludwig of Hesse but he put up his royal guests in a large and fully modernised farmhouse in the village. With snow three feet deep and perfect for a beginner, it would be hard to imagine a more idyllic setting in which to learn to ski. But the tranquillity of the scene was greatly disturbed and the population of Tarasp swelled beyond recognition by the attentions of the world's press.

Prince Andrew comes to grief

Top left: Prince Charles at Klosters

The holiday was nearly abandoned as curious visitors joined the throng who witnessed the Prince's first faltering steps on skis while photographers, thigh-high in snow, were pursued by the royal detective in a suit. Despite such close scrutiny, the support of his cousins Prince Gwelf, Prince Georg and Princess Friederecke helped the Prince of Wales take to skiing from the start. In the able hands of his teacher Guiseppe Heinrich, the Prince had three lessons on his first day. He took a tumble or two, but was said to be 'tremendously keen on skiing'. After only six days on skis, the Prince took his bronze medal for 'mastery of the curriculum of a beginner's course' and passed with flying colours.

Once at his Scottish public school Gordonstoun, Prince Charles went skiing in the Cairngorms with other boys and in 1964 a plan was afoot to bring Herr Heinrich over from Switzerland to teach Prince Charles and Princess Anne in Scotland. Unfortunately lack of snow made this impossible.

In the following year the royal children were not to be thwarted, and with Prince Philip they went to stay with the Liechtenstein royal family at Vaduz. Prince Charles broke a ski while out on the slopes and collided with a photographer, whilst Princess Anne also had her troubles. The Duke of Edinburgh became very annoyed when the foreign press tried to photograph the Princess tobogganning.

In 1966 not only did Prince Charles have a winter holiday with the Liechtensteins but later in the year the Prince went summer skiing on the slopes of Mount Buller, about 150 miles from

The Duke and Duchess of Gloucester at Klosters

Opposite: Prince Edward and friend on holiday in the Italian Alps

Melbourne, during his stay at the Australian school Timbertops, part of Geelong Grammar.

Princess Anne was the first to try a chalet party when she went to Val-d'Isere with a group of friends in 1969 and tested her skills on the nursery slopes. The Princess was chaperoned by the Queen's lady-in-waiting Lady Susan Hussey who said she doubted if the Princess would go out much in the evening as the skiing left her exhausted.

Prince Charles first tried the newly created French ski resort, Isola 2000, on his way to public engagements in Monaco in connection with the Variety Club of Great Britain, before settling for Klosters in 1978. On that occasion he took the Princess of Wales' elder sister Lady Sarah Spencer with him and despite the couple's insistence that they were just great friends, there was speculation of a royal romance. That same year the Prince was made Patron of the National Ski Federation of Great Britain.

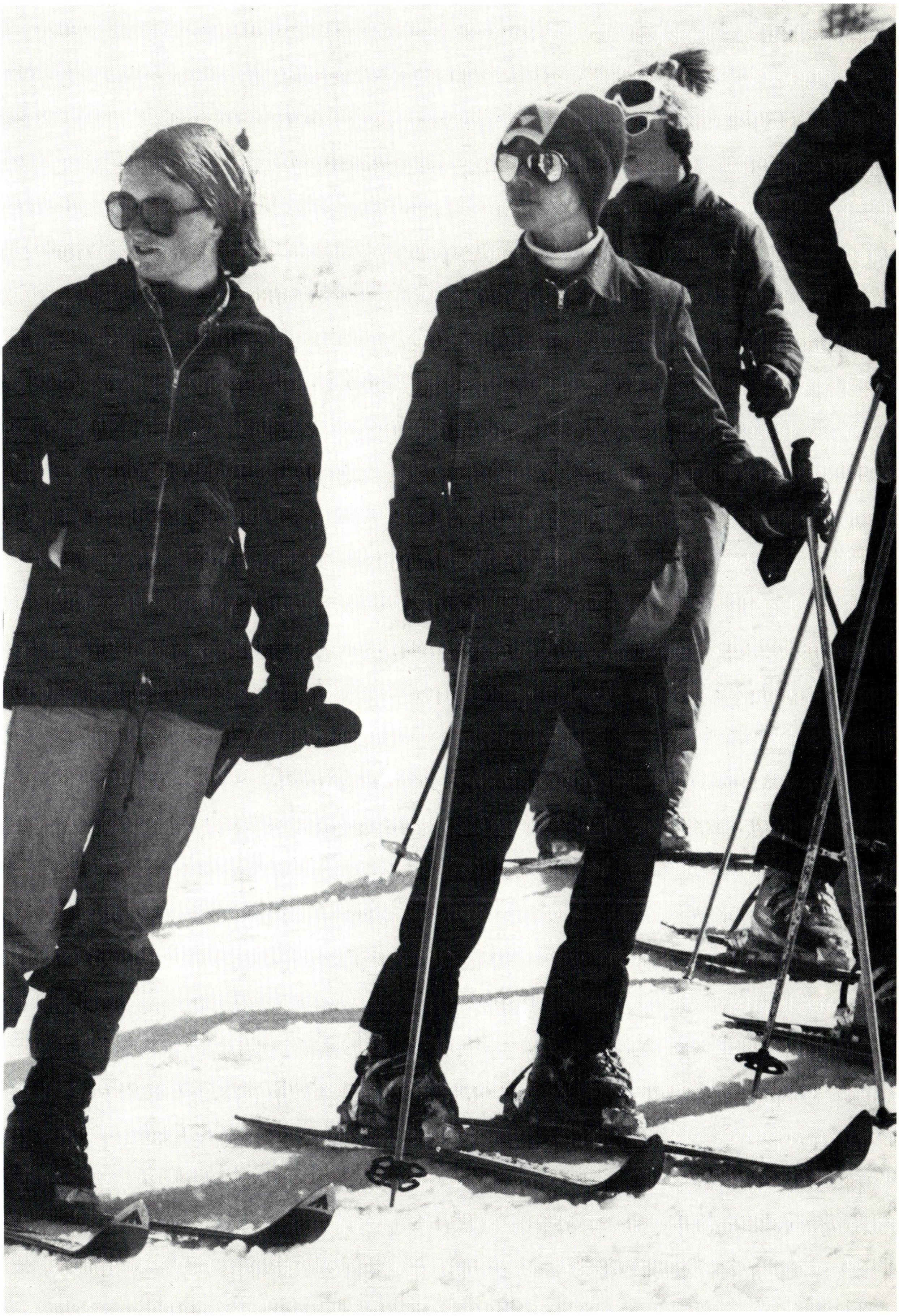

110

Prince Andrew skiing in Canada while he was at Lakefield

The next three years found Prince Charles back in Klosters staying at the chalet of his friend, Charles Palmer Tomkinson, a former Olympic skier. Prince Charles behaves in a characteristically unpretentious way while skiing. He eats a simple lunch in a tourist log cabin on the slopes, and takes his place in the queue for the cable car like everyone else.

Sometimes providence or the Prince takes pity on the press, hard up for a story. One year he disguised himself in a false nose and spectacles, while on another occasion Miss Switzerland – all 34-23-34 of her – mysteriously bumped into him on the wide expanses of the Wolfgang Pass, ten miles from Klosters. Miss Barbara Mayer, for it was she, was momentarily surrounded in a sea of press attention and gladly told the eager reporters that she had come fifth in the Miss World Competition.

Security is also a headache for the skiing Prince. In recent years his police officer has been equipped with a radio so he can keep in constant touch with the authorities while Prince Charles wears a bleeper.

The Prince obviously thoroughly enjoys skiing and recently won the admiration of many when, accompanied by the Duke of Gloucester, he conquered the 'ice wall' at Klosters. The ski run, an 8,000 foot sheer face known locally as *Wanger* is so dangerous that it remained closed for three years.

Prince Charles's younger brothers Prince Andrew and Prince Edward have in some ways been luckier, as they have been allowed to ski in peace, Prince Andrew generally going to Switzerland while Prince Edward prefers Italy and Austria.

Opposite: Prince Charles on the slopes at Isola

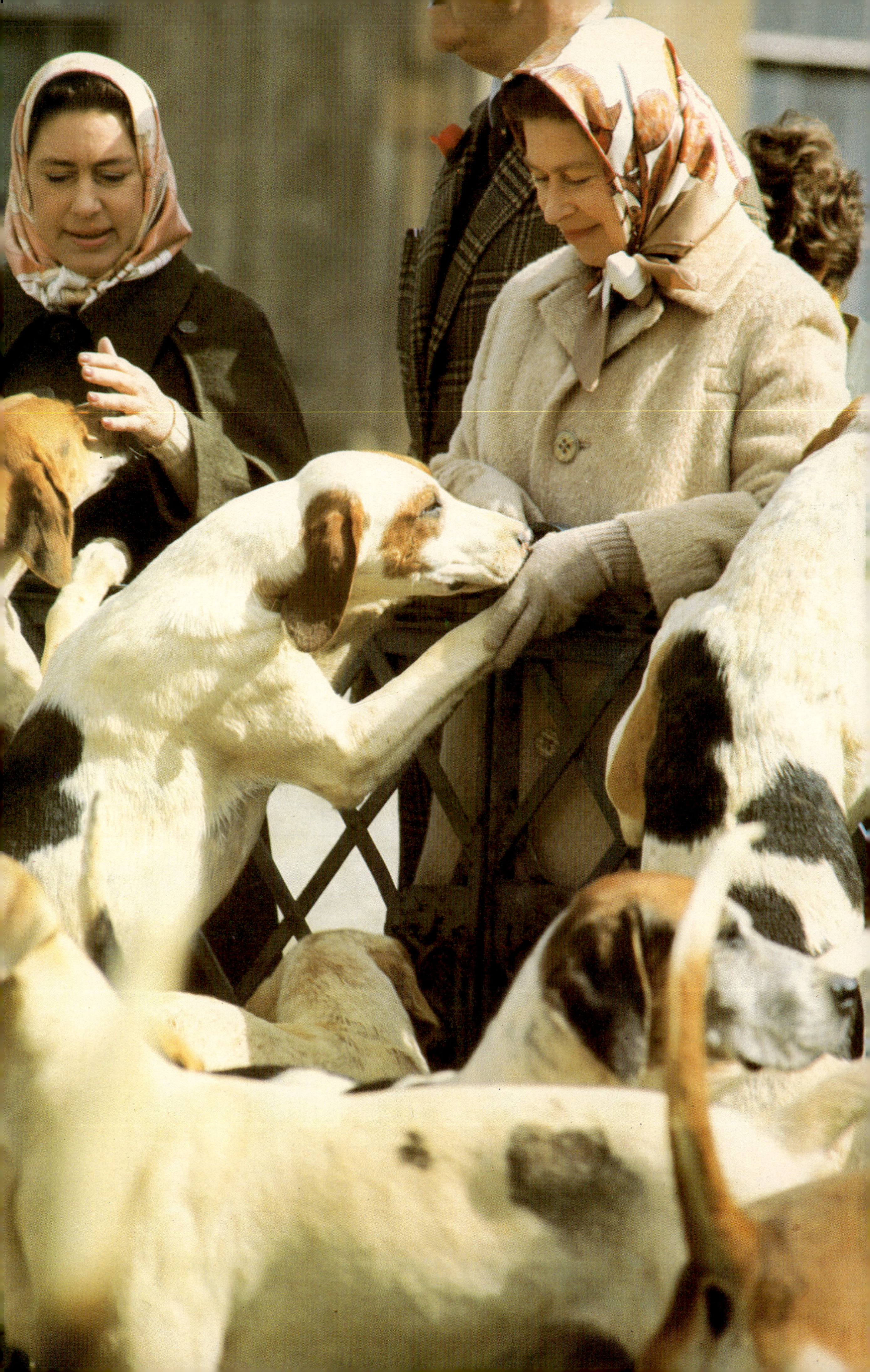

Prince Charles hunting in Cheshire

FIELD SPORTS

AS THE British royal family have learnt to their cost, bloodsports arouse strong passions. Prince Charles was labelled a hooligan after going boar hunting, Princess Anne has had frequent brushes with hunt saboteurs and more recently the Princess of Wales has had to endure the full wrath of the League Against Cruel Sports after going deer stalking.

Whatever the rights and wrongs of the case, the royal family rightly feel that how they occupy their leisure time is a matter for them although they do try to be discreet about blood sports.

Like all families who own country estates they know the need to cull the game is a very real one. If the population rises too sharply many birds and animals will become diseased or die of starvation during the winter. It should also be remembered that foxes are classed as vermin and the alternative methods of poisoning or shooting are far more inhumane.

Opposite: The Queen with the Beaufort hounds

113

Prince Edward shooting at Sandringham

His great grandfather George V half a century earlier

Opposite: Prince Charles with his loader at Sandringham

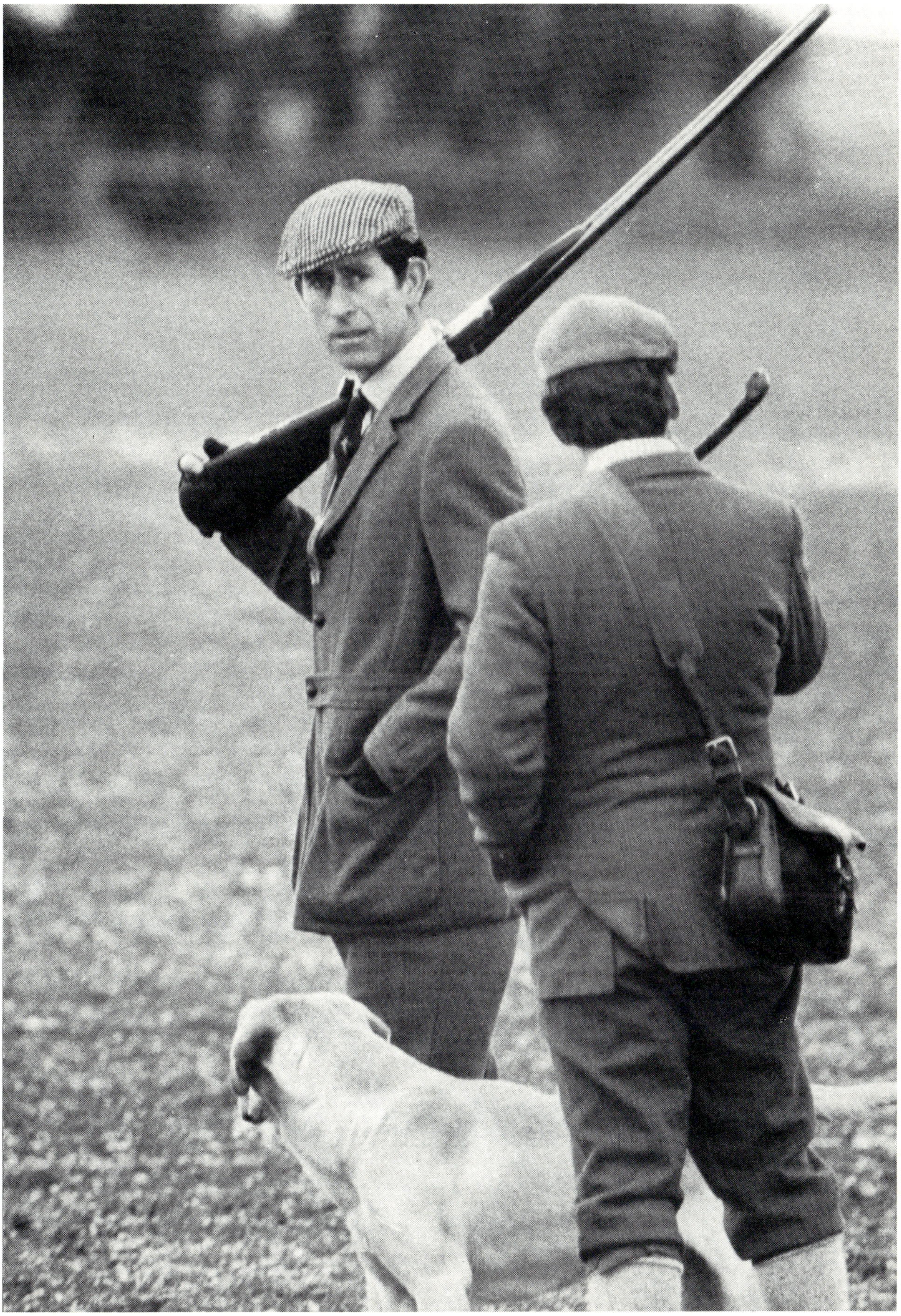

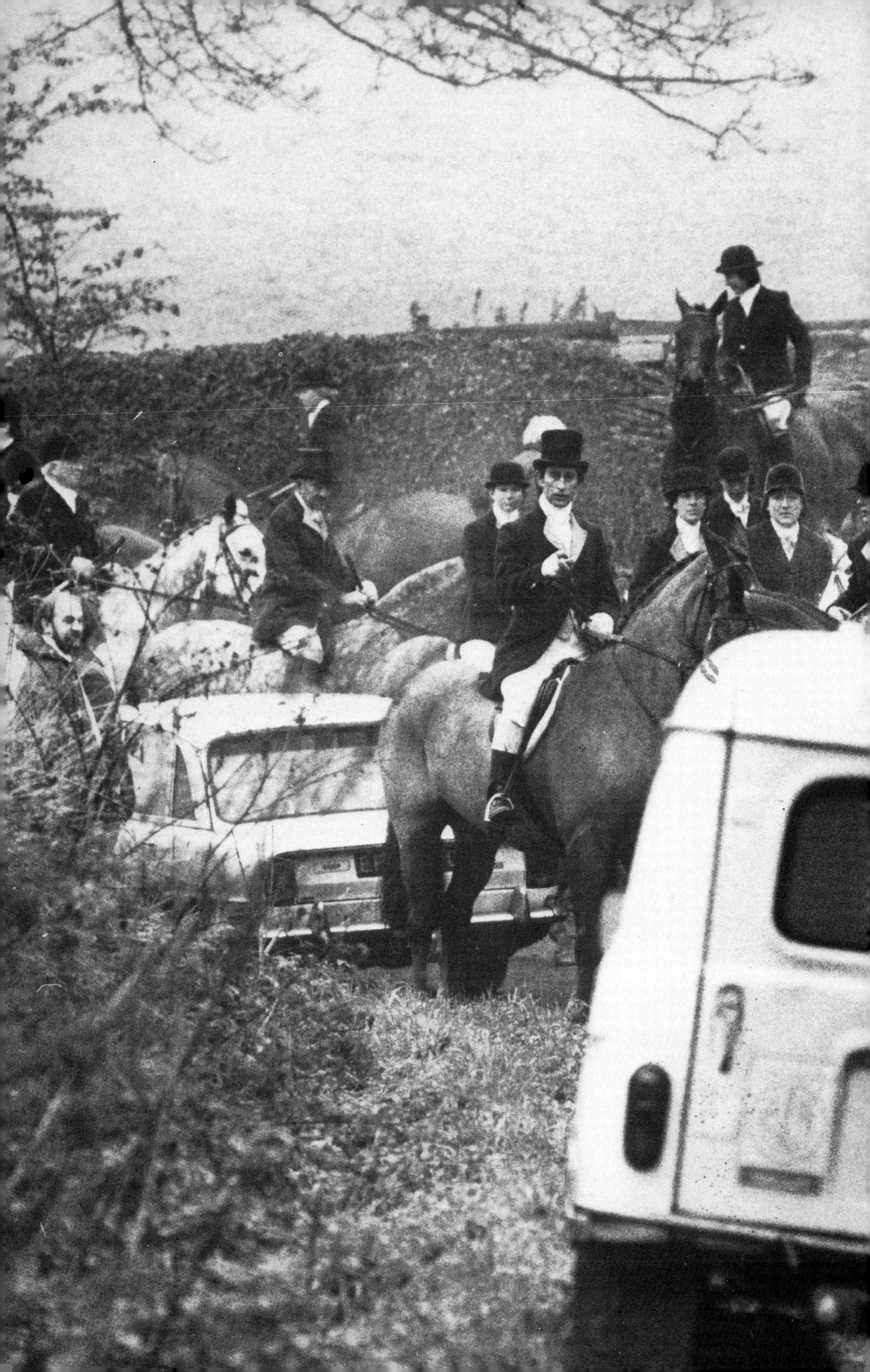

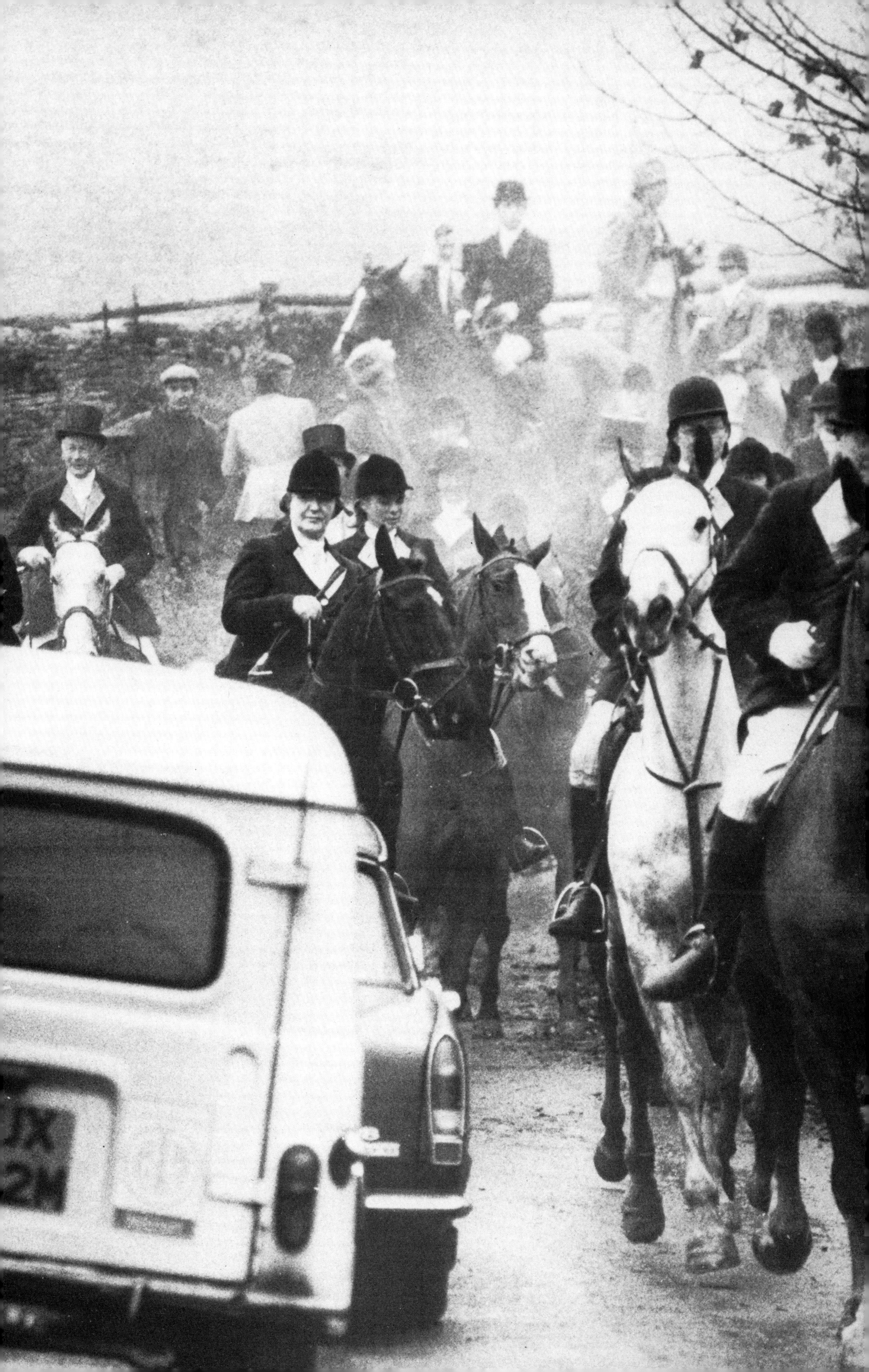

118

Far left: The Prince of Wales bags a wildebeeste in Southern Rhodesia in 1925

Bottom left: A tiger hunt in Nepal organised in 1921 for the Prince of Wales who is on the elephant to the right of the picture

The Queen Mother, then the Duchess of York, in New Zealand in 1927

Princess Anne has been hunting for many years but Prince Charles had his first outing with the Beaufort six years ago. Following in the footsteps of the last Prince of Wales – who was the last member of the royal family to hunt regularly – he thoroughly enjoyed the experience and despite criticism from the RSPCA was out again a week later with the Cottesmore.

Since then he has managed as much hunting as his busy diary of official engagements allows and was in the saddle on his thirty-second birthday.

Prince Charles has said that he believes that hunting is 'a reasonably civilised way' to control foxes, adding: "I have met more British blokes hunting than in any other exercise or sport I have ever done. I very much hope I can go on because in a small way it helps me keep in touch with what actually happens in the British countryside."

Prince Edward has also been hunting but his activities have attracted less attention.

Like past generations of royalty, from King Rufus who died while out hunting in the New Forest 800 years ago, to the late

Overleaf: Prince Charles fishing the Dee

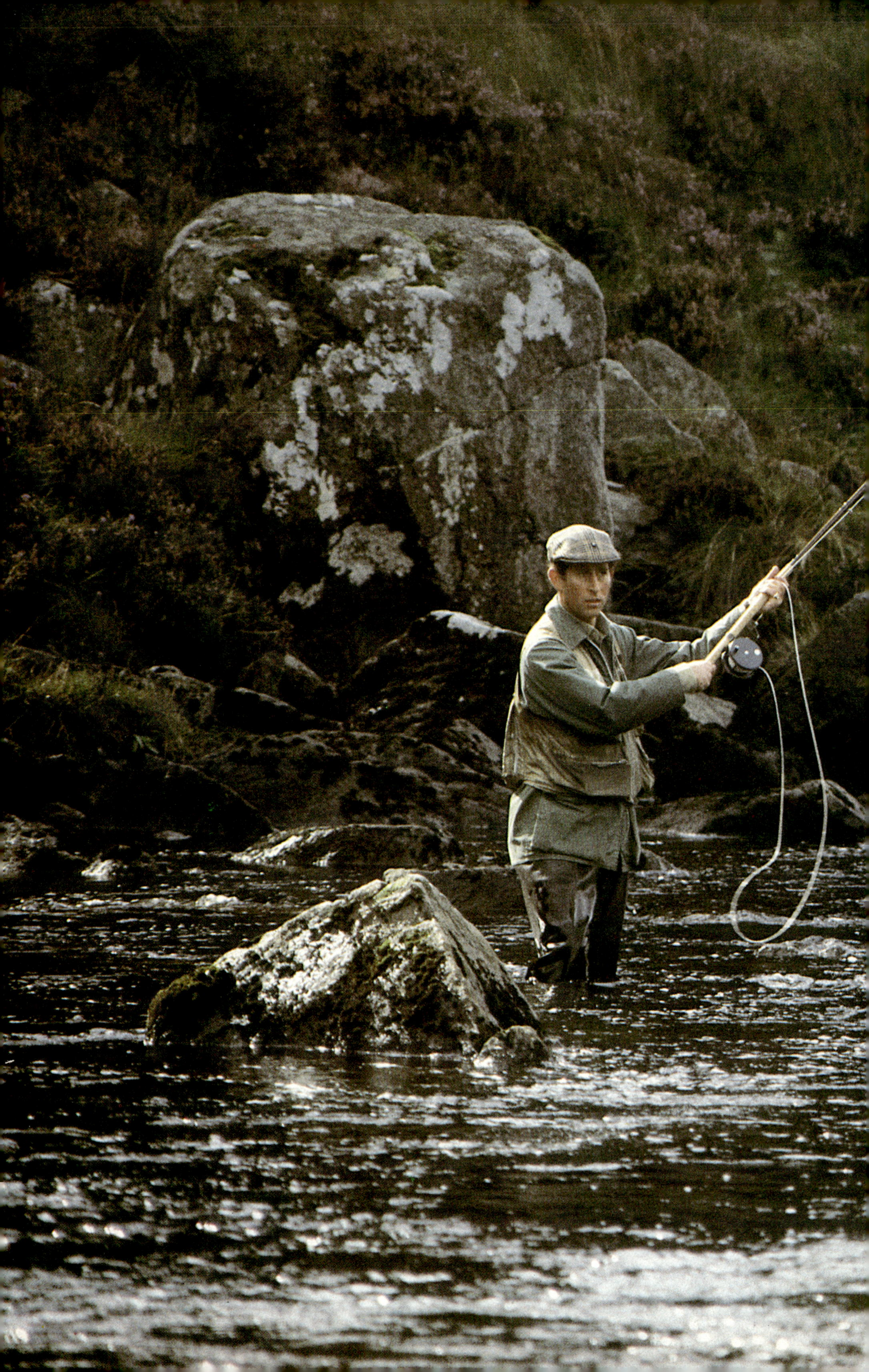

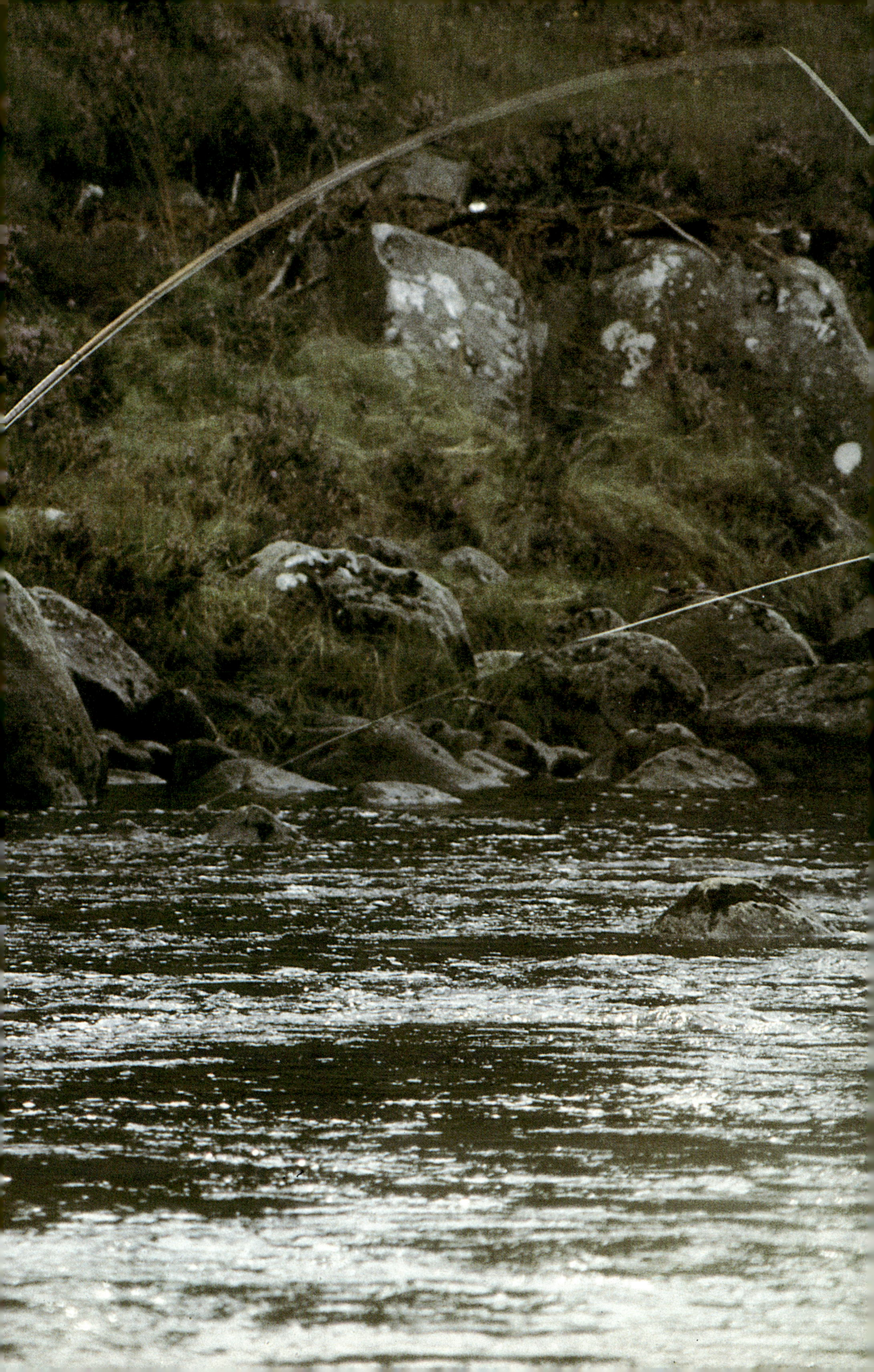

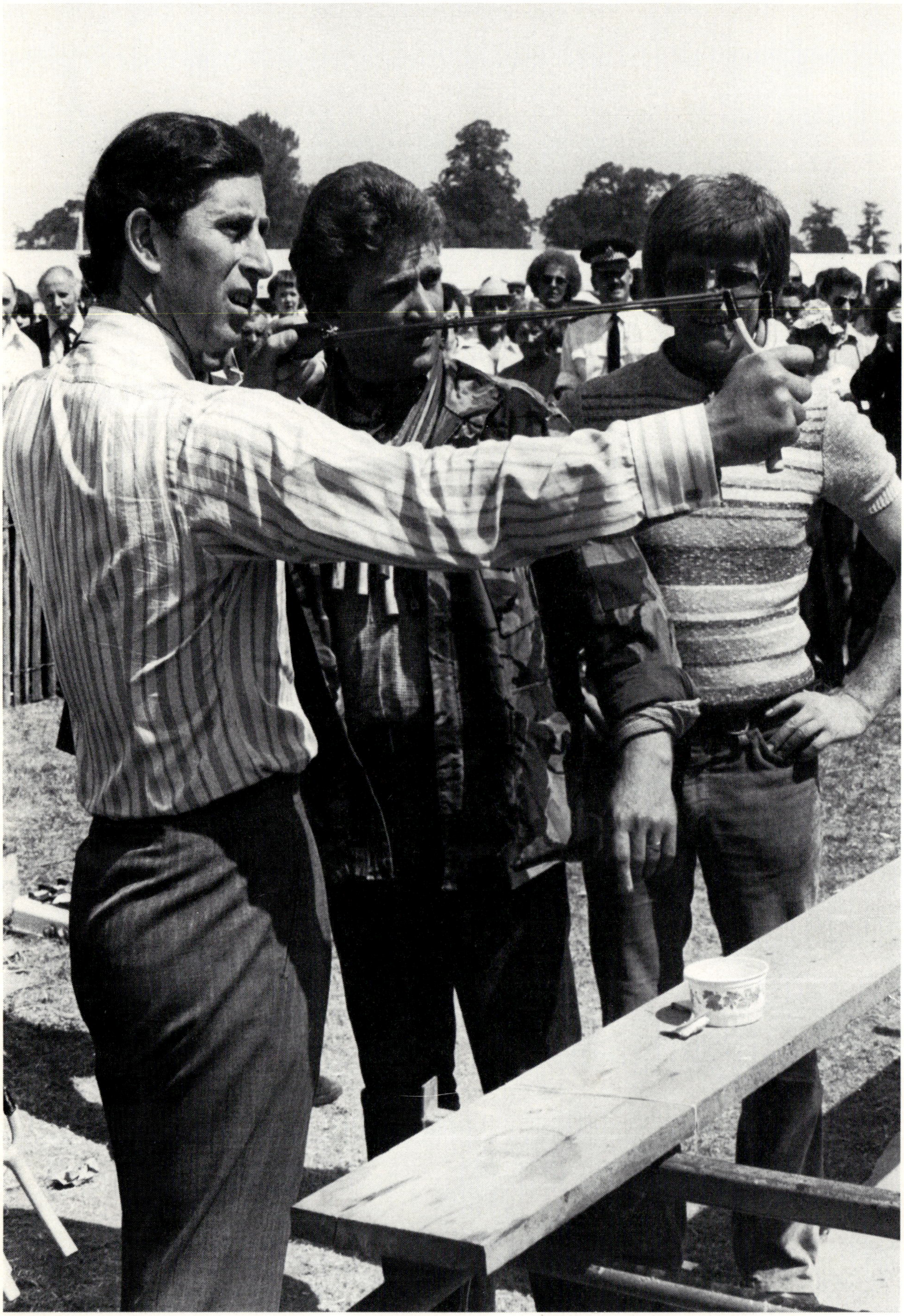

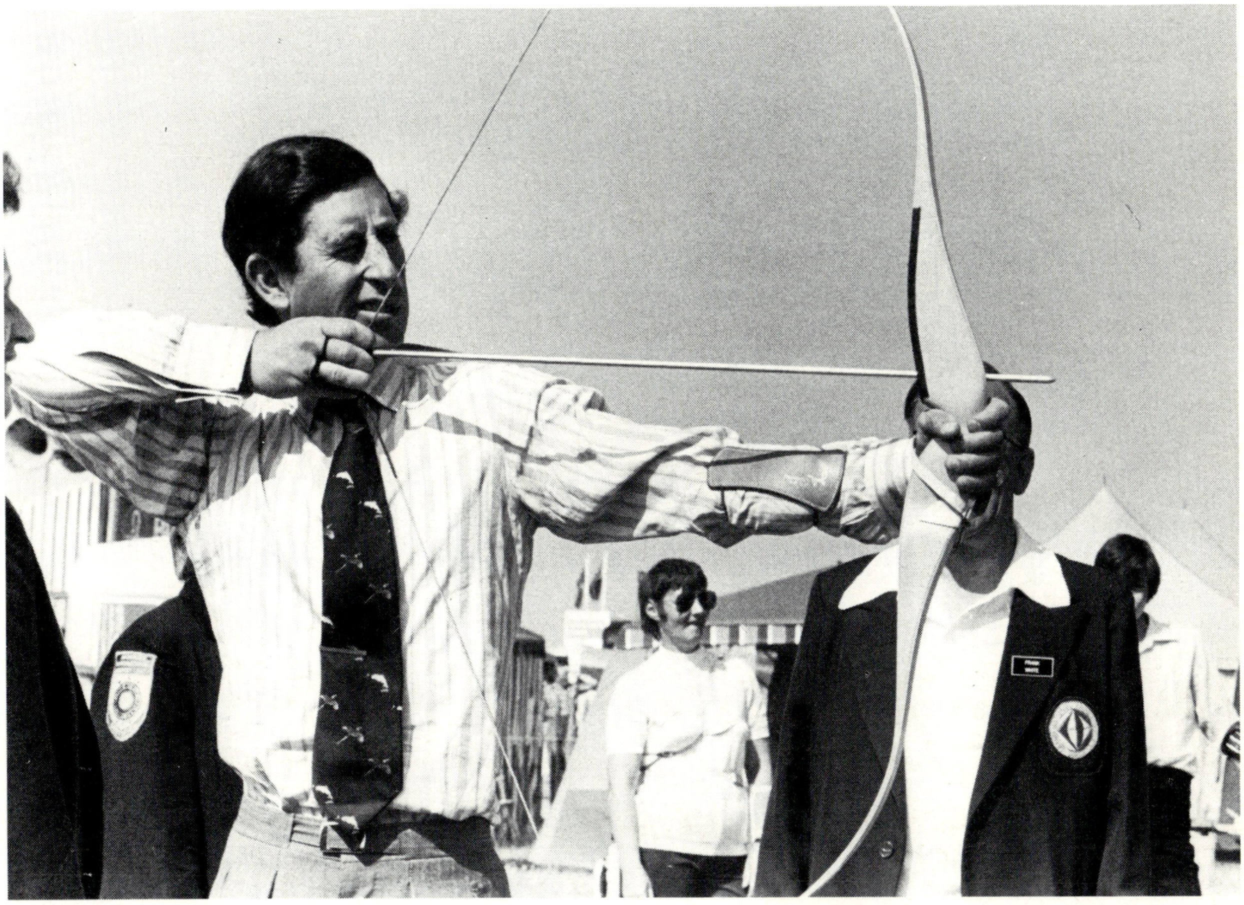

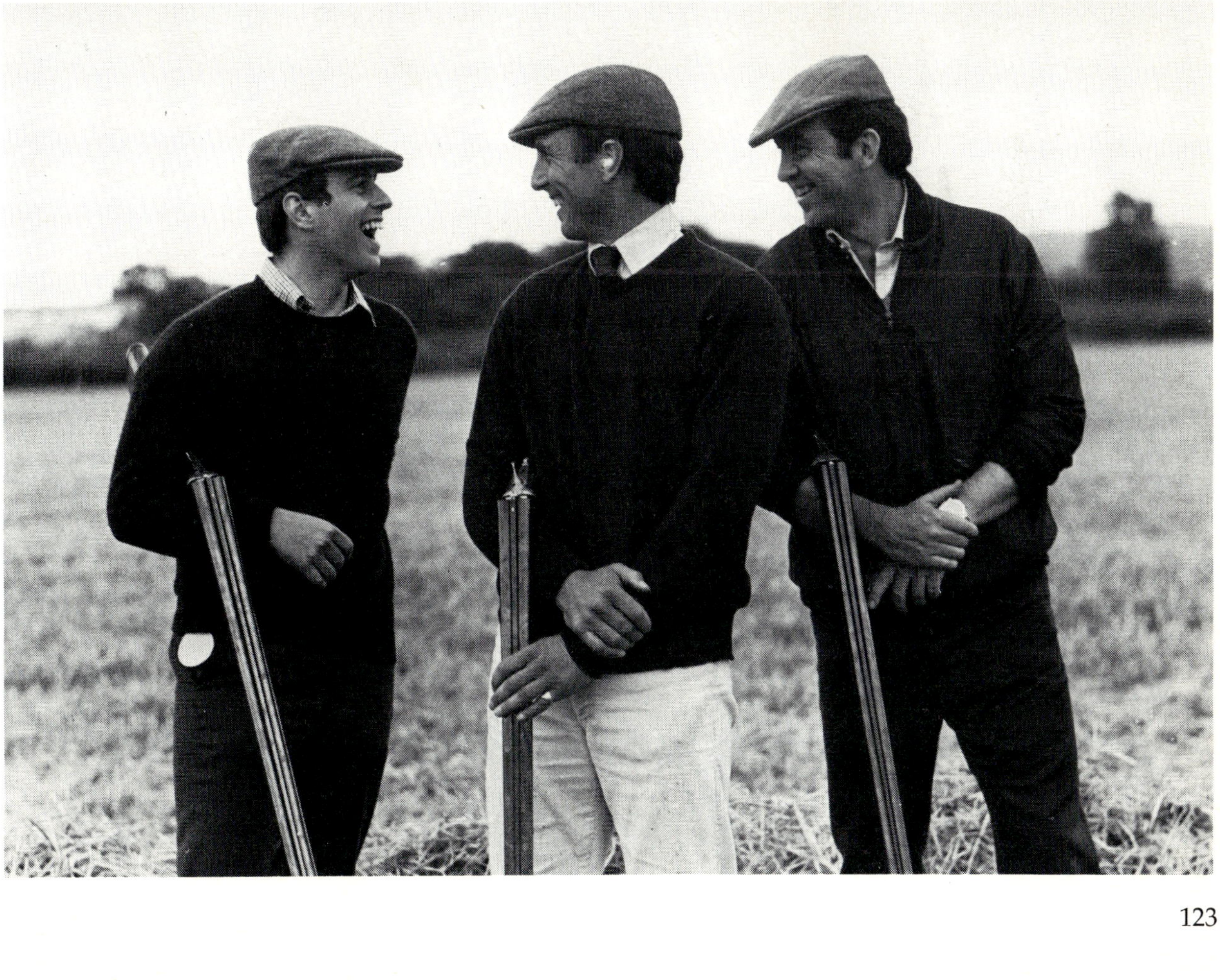

The Duke of Edinburgh fly fishing at Balmoral

Previous pages: Prince Charles with catapult and bow and arrow at the Game Fair and (bottom right) Prince Andrew with Mark Phillips and ex-King Constantine at a clay pigeon shoot

King George VI, the Queen and her family go stalking and shooting on their Balmoral and Sandringham estates.

The Queen, although said to be a good shot, rarely goes stalking, preferring to join the party for lunch.

Some of the royal family do go stalking, as Prince Charles, who is an honorary member of the British Deer Society, readily admits. "I have had more fun watching and stalking deer than I should have believed possible," he once said.

The Prince also tells the story of how he once fooled a large stag with hinds that he was a competitor for his harem. "I advanced over a steep rise with my arms above my head in the form of antlers. The stag took a look and came straight at me, only to realise his mistake and disappear rapidly with a look of profound horror and embarrassment on his face," he said.

Fishing is another favourite royal pursuit. The Queen Mother, who is an expert fisherwoman, frequently plunges up to her waist in the Dee clad in rubber waders.

She has passed on her love of the sport to her grandchildren and Prince Charles even set aside time on his honeymoon at the late

Prince Charles deep-sea fishing off Perth, Western Australia

Earl Mountbatten of Burma's home, Broadlands, to go fishing. Luckily his bride also likes fishing. She learned in Scotland from her mother.

One of the lesser known royal field sports is pigeon racing. Although the Queen does not herself take part, there have been royal pigeon lofts for almost 100 years.

The first lofts were started at Sandringham in 1886 and the first racing pigeons were given to the royal family by King Leopold of the Belgians. These birds were not trained but kept in aviaries, and it was not until seven years later that the then Duke of York, later King George V, decided to start racing. At the same time a loft was also started for his father King Edward VII.

Within six years King Edward VII's pigeons had won first prize in the national race from Lerwick in the Shetland Isles while the Duke of York's came third and fifth.

At the beginning of the First World War it was found that trawlers and drifters engaged in mine sweeping could not communicate with the mainland, so pigeon fanciers were asked to lend birds to the Admiralty for this most important work. The

125

Lady Diana Spencer learning the rudiments of salmon fishing from gillie Charlie Wright

inmates of the royal lofts were immediately volunteered for active service and were later mentioned in despatches.

When King George V inspected the Lowestoft Naval Centre, he sent a message to Sandringham by one of his pigeons.

In 1934 King George V won one of the classic races of the pigeon world – the midland section of the North Road Championships from Lerwick. The King presented five trophies for the sport which shows his great interest in pigeon racing.

The royal lofts had conspicuous success during King George VI's reign. In 1941 one of his pigeons won the North Road Championship from Banff and six years later another won the East Midland section of the championship race flown from Lerwick. In 1951 a royal bird again won the North Road Championship Race from 1414 others competing over a distance of 511 miles.

During the Second World War the royal pigeons again saw

Mr Len Rush, the royal trainer, with some of the Queen's racing pigeons at his lofts in King's Lynn

active service this time with the Royal Air Force. In 1940 one of the King's pigeons brought back a message from the crew of an aircraft which had made a forced landing on the Continent. The bird was given the Dickin Medal for gallantry – the highest award for animals and birds on war service.

The Queen has continued the royal interest in pigeon racing but difficulty in finding experienced staff to care for the loft meant that in 1962 the birds were moved to the home of royal trainer Mr Len Rush in King's Lynn.

Since then Mr Rush has raced the pigeons from April to September and eagerly awaits the Queen's yearly visit to tell her how they are getting on.

The majority of pictures in this book were taken by Serge Lemoine, however the producers would like to thank the following for supplying additional material:
Associated Newspapers, 101, 111; BBC Photos, 32, 35; Camera Press, *v*; Central Press, 23, 26; East Englian Daily Press, 127; Mark Ellidge, 74/75; Tim Graham, 49, 52, 67, 92, 102, 113; Hamlyn Picture Library, 10; Jim Hart, 76; Anwar Hussein, 120/121; Bill Kennedy, 30/31; Keystone Press, 28; Patrick Lichfield, 124; Mike Lloyd, 54, 59, 66; Mike Maloney, 22; Popperfoto, *frontispiece*, 10, 11, 12, 13, 27, 46, 47, 50, 51, 86, 96, 118, 119; Press Association, *vi, vii*, 12, 13, 14, 19, 26, 34, 55, 58, 63, 88, 89, 90, 91, 94, 95, 99, 106, 114, 122, 123, 126; Syndication International, 26, 109, 110